THE NATURE OF DOOR

Door County
Writers and Artists
on Preservation of Place

Edited by Norbert Blei and Karen Yancey
for the Door County Land Trust

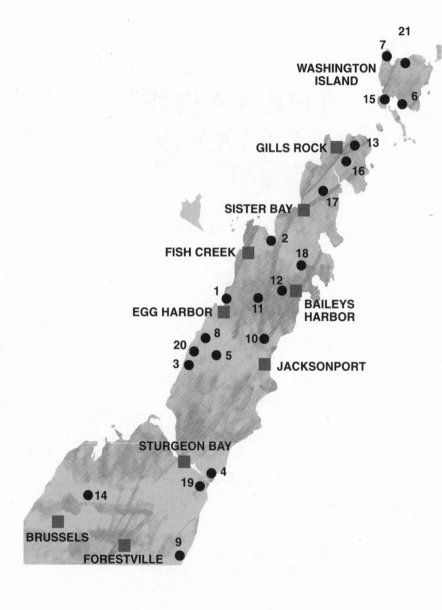

21

7

WASHINGTON
ISLAND

15   6

GILLS ROCK   13

16

17

SISTER BAY

2

FISH CREEK   18

12

1

BAILEYS
HARBOR

EGG HARBOR   11

8

20   10

5

3   JACKSONPORT

STURGEON BAY

19   4

14

BRUSSELS

9

FORESTVILLE

Door County's Irreplaceable Treasures

The Door County Land Trust is working to preserve 20 special places throughout Door County, 20 places which best showcase our diverse and inspiring natural landscapes, our very finest open spaces and wild places. These 20 sites are shown on the facing page and celebrated in the essays and poetry in this book. Proceeds from this book benefit the Door County Land Trust's 20th Anniversary Capital Campaign and ongoing preservation work.

1. White Cliff Fen and Forest Preserve
2. Ephraim Preserve at Anderson Pond
3. Bay Shore Blufflands
4. Kellner Fen Preserve
5. Oak Road Wetland Preserve
6. Detroit Harbor Preserve
7. Little Lake Preserve
8. Lautenbach Woods Preserve
9. Southern Shores
10. Hibbards Creek Preserve
11. Picha Woods at Thorp Pond
12. Kangaroo Lake Preserve
13. Porte des Morts Forest Preserve
14. Brussels Hill/Kayes Creek Preserve
15. Richter Community Forest
16. Gilson-Peterson Forest
17. Door County's Rural Roads Initiative
18. Highway 57 Scenic Corridor
19. Sturgeon Bay Ship Canal Property
20. The Woods at Monument Point
21. Coffey Swamp (a joint DNR-Land Trust project)

This book was made possible by a generous grant provided by Michael and Susan Hedrick through the Fitzsimonds Family Charitable Trust.

Editors: Norbert Blei and Karen Yancey
Layout Editor: Jan Mielke
Cover Art: Dan Anderson
Inside Pages Art: Charles Peterson
Copyright: © Door County Land Trust 2006
Publisher: Cross+Roads Press, Ellison Bay, Wisconsin
ISBN: 1-889460-17-6
Printed in Canada

About the Artists

Dan Anderson

I approach my subject with no preconceived message in mind other than a sense of wonder at what is before me. I am not consciously trying to show a world as flawed or perfect. My photographs are simply very personal responses to a subject that I find to be both very exciting visually and emotionally stimulating. One central goal is to convey this emotional response and the essentials of a subject in my photographs. I look at how a strong sense of light wraps around the form, texture, and fabric of an object, evoking meanings that may be placed onto film. To that end, while many of my photographs may look literal and straightforward, the fact is that if the original subject could be examined, one would see that the print may express a great departure from reality.

I prefer to work in series as it involves me in a subject that requires a period of time and a number of photographs to make a coherent photographic statement that I find impossible to make in a single image. Some series seem to be complete with only a few photographs, while others have many photographs and yet still do not feel complete. Some of these themes, such as the Door County Barn Interiors and the Celebration of Door County Women, I consider finished, while others such as the Sandstone Ballet Series have been themes that I return to again and again over many years.

Charles Peterson

After service in the Pacific during WW II, Peterson trained at Chicago's Art Institute and The American Academy of Art, earning degrees from Marietta College (Phi Beta Kappa) and Ohio University with post-master's study at the University of Wisconsin. He enjoyed a 20-year career as Professor of art and department head at Marietta. In 1985, the college conferred on him an Honorary Doctor of Humanities degree.

In 1973 he took up a new career as full-time painter, moving with his wife Sue and three daughters to Ephraim. He became widely known for his illustrations for *Wooden Boat*, *Sail* and other maritime magazines. In 1987 he was invited to show his work at the prestigious Mystic Seaport Maritime Museum's International Competition, where he subsequently won prizes and is now listed among their Modern Maritime Masters.

In 1989 The White Door Publishing Company began national distribution of his 15-year, 63-reproduction "Memories Collection" which quickly earned him a place among *U. S. Art Magazine*'s list of the top 10 most popular artists in the national print industry.

He has published two books, *Reflections* and *Of Time and Place*, which won the 1997 "Best of Category" award from The Printing Industries of American, Inc.

Table of Contents

Foreword

by Karen Yancey

I stand on a path at Walden Pond in Concord, Massachusetts, on a brilliant fall day in October, 2001, trying to overcome my dismay. Although the pond is majestic, surrounded by a curtain of crimson, okra and amber trees, there is nothing left of the "wild place" that Thoreau wrote about more than a century ago. A Thoreau fan since college, I had come to ponder some of the themes of his book and to witness the landscape that inspired his writings.

But there is no quiet place to reflect here. As I look out on the pond, hundreds of tourists hike its shores on a wide pebbly path made by the state. A souvenir store sits next to a parking lot crowded with tourist buses. I wait in line behind dozens of people to get a peek inside a replica of his tiny cabin. Inside the store, I am greeted by Christmas ornaments made of leaves from the pond dipped in gold and silver paint.

As I wait in line to buy a book on Thoreau, I close my eyes and picture my own "Walden Pond" back in Door County. There I can stand on the one rustic pier jutting out into the lake and see nothing but trees and water and sunlight. I am alone: no noisy traffic, no souvenir shops, no people. I can sit for hours watching dragonflies skim across the lily pads, ease off the pier into the undisturbed water for a quick swim or kayak silently across the pond to the forest on the other side. There are ancient Indian mounds along the lake, mossy and marked only by stones, known only to the local neighbors. Each time I visit here, I literally feel stripped, cleansed of everything that is unessential. I find what I have come to treasure most in my adult life: peace. It is my place, in John Muir's words, "to play in and pray in, where nature may heal and cheer and give strength to body and soul."

My pond is still truly a wild place. Aldo Leopold, one of Wisconsin's most well-known conservationists, defined wilderness back in the 1930s as a "continuous stretch of country preserved in its natural state, open to lawful hunting and fishing, big enough to absorb a two weeks' backpack trip and kept devoid of roads, artificial trails, cottages or other works of men." Using Leopold's definition, there are no vast wildernesses left in Door County where one can trek for days or weeks without encountering another human being, but there are remnants of this wilderness — wild places unmarked by humans where one can go to be alone and feel the harmony and richness of the natural world. These remnants as Leopold defines them are important "degrees of wilderness." They are smaller sites that serve as "representative samples of original wilderness conditions" and "intermittent escapes to uncivilized stretches of land." The need for these escapes, he claims, is embedded deep in the American psyche.

Door County abounds with these remnants of wild places simply because many are hard to access by car, are unknown to a larger population, and have been far away from large urban centers. They have survived 20th century development and tourism for the same reason larger, grander wilderness has survived around the world, such as the Boundary Waters Canoe Area in Minnesota or Rio Bravo in Belize. You have to get to them by foot or by boat and they aren't close to major cities. Wild areas that are easily accessible by car or near large cities, such as Mount Rainier in Washington or Yellowstone National Park in Wyoming have been literally trampled to death by tourists.

Door County is particularly fortunate in that it has so many spectacular areas of natural undisturbed beauty still left as it enters the 21st century and that early settlers and summer residents realized that humans couldn't improve upon them. As *National Geographic* noted in the 1960s, the county is "a place so delicious." Today, there are still countless meadows where a remarkable diversity of bird populations nest and sing. Wetlands ringed by cedar forests teem with baby bass and emerald-green dragonflies, while blufflands known only to neighboring cottage dwellers beckon more bald eagles back to the county. Sand dunes from ancient lakeshores continue to serve as habitat for red fox and other land mammals. As any naturalist who lives or vacations in Door County knows, paradise can still be found here.

But most conservationists can't help but recognize that the clock is ticking faster and faster, and the question for many conservation groups like the Door County Land Trust is how to protect and share these places with lovers of the wild, without having them ruined by all this human attention. There is no easy answer.

For example, as I look at my beloved Door County version of Walden Pond, I know there are tracts of land for sale around it. There have been cabins around this lake for more than 100 years, but the people who built them respected the land and the view of their neighbors and made them small to blend in with the surroundings. Most of the year, they see and experience what Thoreau did 100 years ago. What a privilege. But there is no guarantee that the pond will look like this even a decade from now unless it is protected by a state or private conservation program. In fact, development patterns on the peninsula make it a safe bet that whoever purchases the property for sale will want to put up a 4,000-square-foot home right on the water, not in the trees, so that they will have a better view, or that a condominium developer will try to change the zoning and succeed in rimming the pond with condominiums.

The loss of this irreplaceable wild area will not only be mine. The disappearance of wild places in Door County have a severe cost in terms of the human spirit, the native people, the artistic community, and the scientific world.

Every human being needs to feel a connection to the land, a sense of belonging to a greater natural community. This sense of wonder, this spiritual need, is part of our original equipment at birth and essential to the development of an ethical and moral foundation of both individuals and a community, argues David Orr in his book *Earth in Mind*. Teaching environmental education at my children's school, I have only to accompany my third-graders to the wild prairie to see the joy and connection that many of them experience. It is in this natural place that they learn to watch a spider build its web and not destroy it and to feel the elation of running through acres of Indian grass taller than they are. They literally scream with joy when let loose on the land. It is no different for adults. As the many authors in this book note, it is this love of the land, this sense of knowing the essence of a place and belonging to it, that leads us as well to solace and happiness.

The loss of native landscape destroys native communities. Like the Potawatomie, the original Scandinavian settlers of Door County had learned to make a living that was, for the most part, in harmony with the land by fishing, hunting, shipping, and farming. Over the last century, these livelihoods have gradually disappeared. The children and grandchildren of these original settlers have had to look to other locales to support themselves and their families. Many of these wonderful individuals raised in the county's more untamed days, whom my co-editor Norbert Blei describes in his book *Door Way*, are disappearing with these wild places. Only in a few places in the county, like the more isolated Washington Island, have several generations of families continued to make a living off the land and to sustain a healthy community.

Disappearing natural beauty also destroys a community of artists. The writers, poets, photographers, and painters who have volunteered to participate in this book know how essential these wild places are to their work. Like all artist communities around the world, what has drawn them here is the dizzying array of natural beauty that becomes the focus of their work. Replacing wildlife and scenic beauty with shopping centers, condominiums, golf courses, and tract housing development literally destroys their subjects. Who can write a poem about a shopping center or paint water with condominiums lining the shore? Without their art, our souls starve as well. There is so much at stake than cannot be measured against the economics of the construction and tourist economy of Door County.

Finally, the loss of land in its natural state creates an unhealthy landscape from a scientific perspective. Door County is home to some of the richest biodiversity in the state, including dozen of endangered plant and animal species. Meadows and forests are an important habitat for dozens of bird species, and hundreds more depend on its wild areas as a resting place during their migration. Wetlands around the county serve as habitat and breeding grounds for fish and other aquatic life while replenishing the underground aquifers. Blufflands and shorelines house rare snail species and returning bald eagles. The interrelationship of all of these systems in a wild place remains healthiest if they are left undisturbed.

So given the choice of sharing my wild place or of watching it destroyed by development, I will choose the former. And so would all conservationists. In identifying and publicizing 21 of the wildest places left in Door County in this book, The Door County Land Trust is trusting that the people who choose to read this book and discover these places will have the same love and respect for the wild as the authors who have volunteered to write about them. The Land Trust is also hoping that you will join us in our efforts to protect these lands through conservation easements, land donations, and land purchases. Funds from the Land Trust's 20th Anniversary campaign will be directed to protect these wild places, which have been chosen because of their natural beauty, their unusual landscapes, their value as endangered plant and animal habitats, and their spectacular and irreplaceable vistas.

Once we have protected them, how can we keep them wild? A managed wild place is an oxymoron, yet a small amount of intervention is necessary for continued protection. You won't find highway signs directing you to these wild places. Some are accessible only by foot or boat. These areas won't invite you with picnic tables and recreational equipment. We are not in the park business. There will be small signs to identify them and markers to keep you from trespassing on neighborhood properties. In some cases, the land donors have asked that certain outdoor activities be encouraged and there will be hiking, hunting, educational, and cross-country skiing trails posted.

A book on Door County's wild places would not be complete without an essay on the only true wilderness that is left in the county, Lake Michigan. The lake is perhaps the only place in Wisconsin where a human being can disappear for weeks without human contact. More important, the interrelationship between the lake and the land is inseparable. The lake has created, nourished and shaped the land that is Door County for millions of years and will be the single most important factor in the health of the land in the years to come. A polluted and unhealthy Great Lake will negatively impact many of the wild places we have describe in this book — from the bass nursery in Detroit Harbor on Washington Island, to the Bay Shore Blufflands in Egg Harbor.

Protecting, sharing and celebrating these remnants of wilderness, these healthy wild places that nourish us, is our gift to future generations, and to ourselves.

Homage
by Alice D'Alessio

Come, we'll talk to the trees
the venerable holy fathers

their evening branches hung with crows
like funeral flowers.

Walk softly among my friends
and listen, learn forbearance.

Deep in their cowls their voices
murmur Te Deum, praise the Great Spirit,

the Sun God. Offer thanks to Allah,
to Buddha, to the Great Goddess.

Nodding and bowing, they reach
wide arms in friendship. They do **not**

bloody the soil to prove
whose prayer is best. Listen.

They will grant you absolution. Repent.

On Kellner Fen
by Ralph Murre

The dark and watery eyes
in the center of the fen
are slowly closing;
tired from these years of staring
at the changing sky,
reflecting its fickle moods.
A little rest, a geological blink.
Maybe just a millennium or two.

Tread lightly or avoid altogether the fen. Most of what you've learned is best forgotten if you travel in this otherworld; things you thought you knew do not apply. You're heavier than you remembered. You're walking through a low wood when a perturbed white-tail buck signals the end of *terra firma*, and then you notice that the trees move with each of your footsteps. You remember someone once telling you not to make waves, but you are. You are at sea. In the woods.

It comes to you that you could fall through the surface of this planet, which, until minutes ago, you thought was your own. Maybe, you muse, this wouldn't be such a bad way to walk through life — aware of your impact, aware of the waves you make.

There's a clearing of some sort ahead, just through this thicket of buckthorn covered with berries covered with birds, and all of it, covered with gleeful birdsong. You have to see what's out there, because you've become oddly curious about this dangerous place. It's a lot like something Mother told you to stay away from.

Following alongside a slow stream, darker than night, you emerge into the clearing and, Whoa! You're as startled as the green heron who's just exploded into the air. Before you is a landscape that certainly can't be in Door County, Wisconsin. Somehow, you walked into a woods just out past the lighthouse and now you're somewhere in . . . Canada? . . . northern Canada? You can still hear the surf of Lake

Michigan, but you're afloat on a half-mile mat of sedge grass, surrounded by low trees and teeming with kinds of life you've not seen
often, if at all.

"What's this dark red thing? It's not in my book —and this pink
flower? The leaves remind me of rosemary. Here — the book says this
little purply one is a brook lobelia and that white one is a northern
bog aster. Oh, wow! Look — pitcher plants! They're everywhere!"

In your excitement to look closely at a pitcher plant, you've forgotten the tenuous nature of your footing, and you're suddenly
sprawled and hurting a bit and one of your legs seems to be missing.
You can still feel it, though, and it's cold and wet; it's in another realm
— a watery and, perhaps, bottomless netherworld. Well, the beautiful
pitcher plant is now in your face, and you notice that it's devouring a
hapless insect. You can't help but suppose that the carnivorous plant
is a microcosm of this whole place, which seems to have *you* in *its* di-
gestive tract. Perhaps, you're thinking, I should have listened to Mom.

If you're lucky enough to extract yourself, as I was, and regain
your sea legs, you may still find that this place is hard to leave — your
mind and your camera will be filled with new images, and many of
them unusual enough that they'll require some real study. (Whose
were those wet burrows . . . not very big . . . voles, maybe?) The flowers — they're not *all* going to be in the first two or three books you'll
check. The birds — they're just too quick. You'll need to come back.
You'll need to know how all this looks when these tamaracks are the
last golden flames against winter's dark cold. And what of that first
hint of spring thaw? What's the first thing awake?

You'll need to check things out; hear the stories about how this
place was going to be converted to a commercial cranberry bog.
Maybe you'll run into an old-timer who tells the tale of the planned
frog farm, to supply the burgeoning frog-leg market of the 1920s.
Maybe you'll even meet the land-surveyor, who abandoned an effort
at subdivision when his iron survey stakes fell right through the surface of the "land."

You'll need to wonder about how this word, "fen," sneaked into
America. Was it hidden in the pages of *The Wind in the Willows*, or did
Tolkien make it up, maybe?

When you leave, it will probably be with the reluctance that you
leave a party when you've just met a beautiful, but dangerous,
stranger. And just as you may imagine what life would be like with
that stranger, you may think about how great it would be to build a
little home on the edge of the fen. You could visit every day, start a
journal, be a real modern-day Thoreau. You, after all, have great ecological awareness and could help to protect this jewel. I ask you to

consider, though, before you bring in the bulldozers, the well-drillers, the power lines, whether Walden Pond benefited from the cabin of the original Thoreau.

Consider benign neglect.

Consider not telling your best friend.

You will thank me, perhaps, for having told you of this place which I have not mentioned in more than 30 years. And then, you will damn me — for having told anyone else.

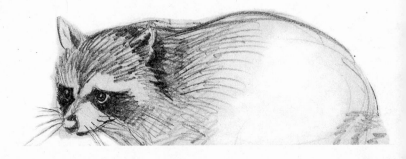

Swamp Song
by Jude Genereaux

There is a cedar swamp outside my door
night wanderings take me to it;
I slide back the heavy window, longing
for the sound of summers past and coming

Steady chirping peepers in black stillness
fill my ears in ringing rising song
soothing empty places;
bullfrogs bong in unison from mucky bunkers
hidden in the dark, their boggy cousins
croon of northern lakes, a pond
   and doors that open in the night.

A deliverance of sound
renews the bond, assuring passage
Grounding me in true home.

Ephraim Preserve at Anderson Pond
by Susan Peterson

These small essays were created from my Bird Journals, 31 years (1974 to 2005) of casual notes about birds and observations of the Anderson Pond area.

In 1973 we moved permanently to Ephraim, Wisconsin. In the woods across the street from our house stands a beautiful open meadow with a pond. This site was the original farm and fields of the pioneer Anderson family. Their small log house, build about 1858, is now a historical memory. For more than 50 years the land has been undeveloped, a natural habitat protecting plants and wildlife.

January 10 1974 The Shrike

I stand near the north meadow of the Anderson property this winter afternoon: total silence, cold still air. Then hear a loud catbird-like call, strange series of squeakings, clucking, attempts at whistling. Find the robin-size bird in a tree nearby. Grayish body, dark mask, strong hooked beak. The "butcher bird." It flies down from a birch treetop to leafless bush, where it pecks at a twig three feet off the ground, then leaves. I walk to the bush, find impaled on the twig the remains of a small creature, mostly bits of meat, feathers. On the snow below is a handful of delicate gray and white feathers sprinkled about. My bird book confirms a northern shrike.

I contemplate this butchery, the delicate graceful birches, the glowing sunset on the snow, and am informed of the way of the world.

I walk back on the meadow path through the falling light, wary of the ice. A pileated woodpecker continues to hammer into a frozen cedar tree. A goldfinch chatters from above. How brutally harsh, and beautiful, these northern winters are. A local man, who is a retired portrait photographer, suggests to us that Door County winters are like a gorgeous woman with long talons of ice.

July 14 1978 The Smallest of Wrens

A winter wren is singing its long lustrous song. I follow the high-pitched intricate series of trills to the Anderson woods, through the cedars, past summer grasses, blue flag, and clumps of asters, down a log-strewn incline to the east side of the pond, the cliff side. (The pond is shaped like a lozenge, with east and west being the long sides.) A beautiful bit of Niagara escarpment, this cliff is covered with large broken blocks of pale dolomite, many rocks set like square tables one can sit on, others tipped with edges jutting haphazardly and tangled with lacy wood ferns, moss, fallen logs, dark snarl of upturned cedar roots, trees reaching skyward.

In this dense wooded glen I find the wren, bobbing from shrub to shrub, then singing again, the loud notes bouncing off the cliff walls, all this coming from a plain brown bird the size of a mouse. The sound reminds me of my aunt's music box with a stuffed bird turning on top, singing long melodious trills and riffs.

I follow the bird south along a faint path that lifts up into a hemlock grove, the cliff now mostly emerald green with a thick covering of moss. The wren gleans what food it can from around the rocks, darting under then out again. It finds crevasses to pick at, tiny rooms to search, a thousand miniature houses under the spill of upturned limestone, under the dark root masses.

Soon the winter wren flies north and disappears. I am content, left standing in the warm shadow of tall majestic hemlocks. A kingfisher rattles across the length of the pond. Red-eyed vireos move through the treetops. I move on the earth below, heading home.

February 1 1983 Raeburn's Painting

We've always called it "the Anderson pond." Of course it is much more than that. It is meadow, gentle hill, stone fence, old apple orchard, wetland, cliff, forest. It is about 30 acres of a natural refuge for wild things, owned by the Anderson family since 1858 when Aslag Anderson bought 110 acres at $1.15 an acre. Cows were watered here. Crops attempted. Barbed wire strung from tree to tree. Apples picked, children born. Some of the logs from the Norwegian settler's small cabin still form a four-foot-high wall in the north meadow. The bleached logs tangled with poison ivy, wild grape, red osier dogwood growing through the center.

We say, "let's ski at Anderson Pond." We — my husband, three girls and I — ski down the path from the gate, through the old field and up the far hill, around a few junipers, following a ski trail into the orchard. Seldom do we ski on the pond. But we still call the area only "Anderson Pond." We did ice skate on the pond a few years back. The year of high water, the spring pond spilling its edge and filling up the surrounding basin, pushing against the cliff on the south end. In the fall, the water retreats to an area half the size of the pond, but that fall the pond was full and froze without wind or much snow. One day the men and children could be heard scraping the fresh snow and frozen leaves off the ice, creating paths around stumps, a large open circle in the middle. Neighbors joined in, a skating party occurred. A happening.

Children played chase for hours around the intricate paths created, the adults skated sedately in the center circle, gliding and turning. I was reminded, that afternoon, of the Scottish painter Raeburn's oil of the black-frocked pastor skating alone on a dark and frozen loch, hands folded like wings behind his back, gliding through solitude.

As the light faded, a small fire was built on the ice, logs were sat on. Conversation floated through the wintry air.

We all felt blessed.

June 4 1992 Listening to Birds

The sound of ravens overhead, their somber and dark language: that and robins are all I hear this early morning. June, 6:30 a.m., sitting on a log, waiting. The light is low and rich, shimmering on the water of Anderson Pond. I can see across most of the pond, although not through a large willow clump near the middle, or grasses and reeds springing up here and there. Natural blinds for the ducks. I wait, hoping to see birds, to hear birds. The waiting becomes a form of meditation; it often does, for absolute stillness is needed. I half close my eyes, pretend I don't exist. Trying to fool birds. A great crested flycatcher breaks the silence with a harsh Wheep! Wheep! Chickadees join in, then the ovenbird sings its loud song from the woods beyond.

And now the ducks appear, slowly at first, as several male mallards float out of cover, green heads glistening. Then the plain tan female appears along the far edge, in and out of hiding, with a trail of small ducklings. She reminds me of a Muslim woman in a brown burka, dodging in and out of the marketplace. At the other end of the long pond are several wood ducks, the brilliant orange, rust, green males slowly turning in place, aware. Kings of color. A small elegant pair of hooded mergansers are often here, but not today.

Other wild creatures greet the expanding day. A frog chirps, a

muskrat crosses the water. A peewee, a swamp sparrow, then a black-
throated green warbler sing their morning rounds. A raccoon waddles
home. Tree swallows circle above the pond, filling their airy space
with liquid notes. A painted turtle suns.
Meditation is over. The world's alarm clocks have sounded.

April 212001 Owl

It was at the south end of the spring pond that I watched a barred
owl take a bath. Leaning against a tree, and with binoculars, I watched
a hermit thrush splash in a small overflow pool, and tiny migrant
warblers drop from a bush into the water and bounce back.

Then the owl silently flew into view. Landing gear lowered, it
dropped onto a branch three feet over the pool, which effectively
cleared the water as birds scattered, mallards paddled north. Master
of the foot-deep pool now, the owl eased into the water and sat for 10
or 12 seconds, as though soaking. This was followed by vigorous
splashing with its wide tan wings, dipping its large round head over
and over, making sure the watery immersion was total, like a Texas
baptism.

Then it hopped back on the branch and briskly shook its feathers
free of water, creating a wide halo of mist. After a brief pause, as
though considering flight or immersion, it was back into the water, an
equally vigorous splashing, a quick hop out of the water, a shake, and
then the owl, like a soft whisper, glided into a hemlock grove and was
gone.

I have never seen an owl take to water before, and never expect to
see it again. In a birdwatcher's life it fits into the category of rare. Or
incandescent. Or holy.

Miracle
by Sharon Auberle

"Perhaps we have been given our oversized minds as consolation for being grounded. Though we have no wings to lift us up, we have imaginations that will. "   —Frans Lanting

Whatever you do in this life,
never ignore small miracles
like this flock of white pelicans
soaring in circles overhead,
their great bodies backlit
by the sun, radiance pouring
down through their wings
in waterfalls of light.

Consider there might be
angels among them,
but even if you don't find angels,
know your heart has been softened
by these immense beings of grace.

Please do not dismiss such gifts,
for rarely are we so blessed.
And oh, don't turn away
and resume your small life,
instead, rise up, for a little while
as if you had seven foot wings,
as if you realized, finally,
we are *all* made of light.

Place and Time
(Coffey Swamp)
by James Olsen

At the age of 12, I was told of a 14-foot man discovered hanging from a tree. A hunter with his dog had penetrated deep into a swamp just east of Sturgeon Bay and a quarter mile inland of the Lake Michigan shore. The tall man they found had gone to a place of the greatest anonymity, taken his own life, and then spent the following years stretching out in the sun and the cold, unfound. I was hooked.

In June of 1974, the Italian architectural critic Bruno Zevi gave an opening speech to the IX Congress of the Italian Jewish Communities: *Hebraism and the Concept of Space-Time in Art.* His thesis was the seemingly irreconcilable cultural gulf between a Greek classical legacy of space and an Hebraic tradition of time. "It has been said that Hebraism is a concept of time, that while divinities of other peoples are associated with places and things, the God of Israel is a god of events, and that the Jewish life, nourished by the Book, is permeated with history, that is, with a time-related consciousness of human tasks. [...] During six days of the week we live under the tyranny of things in space; on the Sabbath, we put ourselves in tune with the sanctity of time." His understanding, in particular of the Jewish artist, was of one in great tension, with no space on earth free of danger, even in the homeland of Israel, attempting in art to reconcile this divide. A graduate student of architecture reading this essay, I had discovered an odd explanation for a boy's fascination with a 14-foot man and a swamp so deep he would be left to grow to that stature. It had to do with this "tyranny of space" and places lost to man, free to live more temporally.

My father would take me from school early on the Friday before Thanksgiving. He would have the 26-foot double-ended coast guard whale boat packed with our hunting gear and provisions for the week, and we would set off from our dock in Sturgeon Bay for the passage up the west coastline of Door County and across Death's Door to Washington Island. It was the deer hunt. My mother's clan would gather there and hunt together on the east side of the Island

and the land my great-grandfather and his brother had settled.

They had emigrated from southern Norway in the last half of the 19th century. Dispossessed as younger brothers, they crossed the Atlantic to New York along with others from Denmark and Iceland who made their way to a small island in the great inland sea of Lake Michigan. These sons and dottirs of Gunnar and Bjarn, Hans and Eric cleared land to farm, built homesteads and boats with the logs harvested and fished the abundant waters surrounding the island for whitefish, lake trout, burbot, herring and chub. Siblings and extended family would be sponsored for immigration as homes and fields were cleared and made ready for their occupation. In this way my own family spread around the west and southern edge of a great swamp. It lay in the northeast corner of the Island, surrounded by marshland.

In their vigor and haste, these men and women carved out usable spaces from the swamp's perimeter. They fenced its edges and turned their backs to it with every structure. When more land ultimately was needed for cultivation, they did what advancing civilizations have always done … drained the swamps. So a deep creek bed was cut through the layered limestone ridge at its northern border with Lake Michigan and its water released, drying up the surrounding marshland. The rich, underlying organic soil was quickly farmed and the swamp, its outer defenses breached, retreated inward. I suspect that a change occurred then in the substance of its forest. What must have been a more open progression of low wetlands likely gave way to a new perimeter of woodland, springing up and growing quickly in that same revealed soil. This is present now as a mature forest of surprising variety. Dense and uniform stands of cedar give way to a block of ash so gray and anonymous in the late fall it seems an unmarked cemetery. In a short walk this changes to a deep growth of mixed hardwood with occasional tall white pine and the old hemlock whose brothers and sisters framed the Midwest. In fact, the experience of the swamp is in part this sharp shift in flora and composition every 50 steps.

So a boy, dressed in red, carrying a World War II German 8-mm rifle would be lined up by his father and given a direction to walk, silently, with a relative within 50 yards or so on either side, plunging parallel into these perimeter forests. At some perpendicular line ahead, a stationary setting of relatives waited for us to convince the deer who lived in that region to move on. It was a geometric, a Greek exercise, imposed on that tangle of woods. I often wished to wander a bit and follow my instincts into the darkness within. The swamp itself, by reduction and legend, had become an impenetrable darkness. Its name, Coffey, donated by an Irishman from County Clare and his family of 13, had evolved appropriately on some maps to Coffee: black, rich, and bitter. When my mother, raised on its southern edge, heard that her son had made his way through its perimeter tangle, she fearfully chastised my father. I kept my desires quiet.

Her fears were based on many stories of cattle breaking loose and running to the swamp, never to be recovered. Or of a horse team, suddenly caught in a mire so complex that only many men collaborating and their horses could extract them. The baseline for this fear was summarized in a single, compelling phrase: quicksand. Now, real quicksand has hydraulic movement, as in a hidden and upward curling spring. I imagine that what these beasts encountered was the deep suspended organic matter of the bogs within. A bog is stationary, but no less inviting and adhesive than the quicksand that came to represent it. The possibility of a hideous sinking death served to draw a Greek line around the swamp and leave it, then drained to a manageable level, to heal its wounds. The life and history of Washington Island grew up around it; a grid of roads, schools in each quadrant, churches, stores, docks, ferries, ice houses, taverns, even a bowling alley. The lives of the Islanders as for us all were both rooted in and defined by these developments; rationalist.

A difference, by reason of isolation, was that the Island retained a remnant of the ancient cultural tradition of oral history. Story-making was still honored there in a poignant way; stories surrounding the swamp were often tinged with bitterness: a settler on the northwest corner, his only remnant several ancient apple trees and a small clearing, dragged to his death by a horse team he had mistreated; a great-uncle, father of 12 and son of the immigrants, looking to make his fortune boiling down the livers of burbot (commonly called lawyer) for a vitamin/mineral-rich oil, ruined by the discovery of an even greater richness in the liver of shark. A compelling set of log ruins set just back from the stone shore in the protection of the cedars on the swamp's north edge was named the Dutch village. One can stand within those few small rectangles and conjure a life of boats rolled up the stones and back, fishing the exposed waters to the north. And then a subsistence life barely cloaked by the cedars, the great swamp just behind, carried on quietly until the wind blew in from the northwest. More than once, I have stood there and imagined a desperate and cloistered love.

The only story I have heard of the swamp with some joy, other than of successful hunts, was of my mother and her sister going down into the hardwoods and near the edges and picking trailing arbutus and orchids of different types to bring back for decoration of the cabin for the holidays. Of course the idea of young girls picking these most

rare of flowers for decoration is now anathema. They found them
commonly. And we still might, except that the whitetail herd has
grown so prolific that it consumes the natural flora as low and high as
it can in these surroundings that are home to it. I would imagine these
rare plants to be especially tasty.

As a boy and then a young man I respected admonitions to stay
out of the great swamp. I would encounter it, dressed in the required
red and then orange of the state, hunting its edges, always drawn to
its density-rich coffee, black and bitter. A good friend and his brother
and I had for several years walked through pine plantations to its east
edge and hunted the hardwood border. Then a season came when I
could not make the pre-Thanksgiving opening weekend, and caught
the last ferry the following week in a northwest storm, growing in in-
tensity. My two friends had come across several days before. We
bunked into our cabin in West Harbor that evening with the wind
howling and the snow swirling past the windows.

At 5 a.m. I knew we were facing a memorable day. The wind and
snow had become relentless, and the temperature fallen into the teens.
As we made our way through the pines and to a ridge at the dark
edge of the outer shell, we were instructing his brother in the direction
and points of orientation for his making way to our customary stands.
My friend and I, however, would enter the swamp in that great storm.
It was calling. If we were Greeks, this was the sirens' song to the great
Odysseus. As his brother quickly disappeared, ghostlike into the swirl
of snow, we quietly acknowledged that we should have said good-
bye. We headed in.

I could not give a narrative of that day with any sequence. We
entered the swamp armed, and soon put up our guns. Snow so light
it swept around us as we walked fell densely, so that we came upon
things as in a fog. This included deer, sometimes in groups, others
alone, and one standing on its rear hooves and reaching up into the
cedars for a morsel. Their experience of us I imagine was much like
ours of them: animals wandering in a wonderland. We came to bogs
and crossed them on young ice. The thick web of roots and stems that
floated on the bog's edge would sink a bit and screech as the ice net
buckled with our weight. We found peninsulas with hardwoods looming up out of the snow, unimaginable in that soggy middle. Trees were
blown down, their shallow roots lifted whole with a full and intricate
pattern of thin limestone torn from the earth; a vertical patio. In stands
of cedar, each nearly two feet thick, the green moss at their toes glowed
in the diffused light. We broke through those cedars onto the north
shore and the wind stripped our breath away. It had the force and
scream of a hurricane. Docks and seawalls all over the great lake were

succumbing to its force that day. It blew us back to the cedars and we slipped into their protective arms. In 20 feet, it was as though one were in a room and the wind occurring outside. We were not walking so much as falling forward, every several steps hooking onto limbs and stones and trunks beneath that snow. It simply rose within the swamp that day, measured by its progress above the knee. Falling became so constant that we finally nearly swam out to the east and found the brother, up a tree. Our way back to the cabin was in darkness, and for two more days we bunked in while the storm exhausted itself.

A few years later, I read the essay by Zevi and knew in some way that it explained that day's adventure. We had left behind a structured spatial world and entered unwittingly one that thrived apart from those constrictions. Slow and stumbling travelers, we encountered elements of its identity within a shroud, surrounded by violence. It was both an encounter with a great storm and the swamp's protection from it, a storm like countless others it had welcomed and thrived on.

I have entered that wondrous place many times since. It has always been a redemptive return. The private wish I have is that it not be protected, certainly not by a government agency whose administrative skill allows a great lake to become a liquid desert for its native species. Nor do I envision it preserved with genteel points of access and brass plaques. I wish it to be ignored, our backs turned to it forever as it deepens, and then perhaps for another great storm to twist and tear apart the forest that surrounds it, let it lay those trees down in a weave so dense and high that even the greatest athlete among the whitetails would move to higher ground. The remnant of those exotic flora might then sense that they are somehow safe and spring up, waiting for nothing.

Let all of us, measuring and constructive Greeks, ignore this darkness, until a soul or two, compelled by its intrigue, attempt to venture in. And if they penetrate it and perhaps fall through the tangle onto a spongy mat of bog grass, let them look down as the water rises on the arms and legs, and see the terrified silver dollar eyes of a long-horned cow beneath the surface, perhaps a beast of ancient vintage just below. It is this kind of place. Enter it not a Greek, but a Hebrew, wandering through time.

Coffey Swamp
by Jens Hansen

Near the North shore of the Island,
Two stones'- throw from the beach,
Coffey Swamp, a jewel of nature,
Lies beneath my feet
Between the beach and Coffey marsh
Lies a modest ridge,
A ridge with cedars tall and straight.
That's where Dutch settlers lived.

Early farming immigrants,
Some from my own clan,
Breached the ridge to drain the swamp
To cultivate more land
This was a hundred years ago.
The swamp's seen little change —
Plants and wildlife, nature's balanced, harmony, sustained.

I smell the earth of Coffey Swamp
Like freshly cut mushrooms
A scent that's mellow, brackish, dirty, musty like a tomb.
Yet new life mixes with the old and ages in between.
The plants and animals live and die,
And new life comes from seed.

The pitcher plant lays well concealed upon the marsh's floor.
Its vessels serve to capture bugs and rain that it can store.
Like baby birds awaiting food their mouths are open wide.
The tiny hairs inside the flutes trap unsuspecting flies.

Sphagnum moss is soft and warm to lay on when it's cold
Or in shade from summer's sun under a cedar grove
Petals, leaves, and thickets are shelter from the storm,

Camouflage amongst the boughs while young are being born.

The morning sun shines golden brown off tall canary grass;
The gentle breezes sway the stalks and wave as I creep past.
Their rustling leaves seem to whisper, listen and you'll hear
A symphony of nature's voices singing loud and clear.

The rain erodes the dark swamp earth from roots of fallen trees.
The dirt caked in amongst the roots eventually falls free.
From the dirt a worm is snatched by a chickadee or wren.
A hawk dives down to catch a mouse whose life's about to end.

A pileated swoops and lands and cocks his head to hear
The sound of bugs beneath the bark, and where to dig is clear.
He's common here but rare they say; he's huge as woodpeckers go;
When silhouetted against the snow his form is proud and bold.

The swamp is seldom shared with man; lore of Coffey Swamp is old
Tales of quicksand swallowing horses make the blood run cold.
Trolls, elves, and goblins could be, have been, seen I've heard;
It's all the myth of Coffey Swamp passed down for generations by
word of mouth.

The Sturgeon Bay Ship Canal Ridge and Swale
by Roy Lukes

It was in the early spring of 1938 that a small group of seven strong environmental visionaries got together to lay out an ambitious plan to conserve the wildflowers of Wisconsin as a valuable natural resource. Up to that time no one in the state had come up with serious proposals recommending wildflower conservation.

One of this "Group of Seven" was Dr. Albert Fuller, a young botanist with the Milwaukee Public Museum who in 1937 had led the fight to save the wildflower-rich ridges at Baileys Harbor and to help form the Ridges Sanctuary. Others in this historic group were Dr. Norman C. Fassett, UW-Madison, one of the country's leading botanists, writers, and strong promoters of helping more people learn about wildflowers; Dr. E. M. Gilbert, UW-Madison botanist; Dr. Aldo Leopold, UW-Madison, who in 1949 had his famous book, *A Sand County Almanac* published; Norman Roeder, Milwaukee Public Museum; George F. Sieker, a Madison attorney who wrote the constitution for and helped found the Ridges Sanctuary; and John Curtis, at the time a botanist research student of Waukesha and who, in 1959 as a UW-Madison botany professor, had his famous book, *Vegetation of Wisconsin*, published.

This broad-minded group was intent on encouraging people to become more community-minded and to help citizens throughout the state to awake to the high value of their wildflowers and other natural resources, considered by these seven men to be "potential gold mines." One by one, these men toured the state working to interest local clubs and organizations in realizing what treasures existed in the form of native plants.

It was Dr. Fuller, who had become very familiar with the wildflowers of the Ridges Sanctuary while researching the native orchids of the state, who emphasized the point that some of the wildflowers of the various areas were so rare as to be found only in Wisconsin. The Ridges Sanctuary at that time was the only known statewide site for several species such as the ram's-head lady's-slipper orchid, small

round-leaved orchid, northern spikemoss, dwarf lake iris, arctic prim-
rose and the northern commandra.

Later in the spring of 1938 the Group of Seven met with the lead-
ers of the Wisconsin Academy of Sciences, Arts and Letters to help
forge the beginning of some type of land preservation group in Wisconsin. Thus was formed the Wisconsin State Scientific Areas group,
later to become the Wisconsin State Natural Areas group. The state
legislature in 1951 established the Natural Areas Preservation Council
for the preservation of scientifically significant areas. Later this was
changed to its present designation of the Natural Areas Preservation
Council. Little did this influential Group of Seven realize when they
began their preservation work that in future years the outstanding
Natural Areas concept in Wisconsin would become a model for many
other states in the country to follow in starting their own programs.

The first scientific area to be established in the state was Parfrey's
Glen. The Ridges Sanctuary became #17 in the state and Toft Point
#57, in 1967. By 1976 the Toft Point Natural Area had grown to 743
acres. The Ridges Sanctuary Natural Area had grown from 40 acres in
1937 to about 1,100 acres by 2005.

Today, people of Door County should feel very proud and fortunate that a total of 21 State Natural Areas exist in Door County. They
range in size from the relatively small 70-acre Jackson Harbor Ridges
on Washington Island, established in 1973, to the large Mud Lake
Wildlife Area of 1,060 acres, designated in 1975. What is of immense
importance is that all of these natural areas are intended for the managed use of the public, for valuable research and educational use, for
the preservation of genetic and biological diversity, and for providing
benchmarks for determining the impact of use on managed lands. Of
utmost value is that these areas will continue to exist for the benefit of
future generations of people, wild plants, and animals.

Today I look in retrospect to the valuable education and temper-
ing I received by working so closely with several of the prime movers
in establishing the Ridges Sanctuary — Dr. Fuller, Emma Toft, Mertha
Fulkerson (who managed The Clearing at Ellison Bay for many years),
George and William Sieker, and Olivia Traven. Every one of these stal-
wart people had the tenacity of a bulldog and never wavered in the
fight to save the Ridges and to make it grow in membership, area, and
importance.

During my 27 years of managing and serving as chief naturalist at
the Ridges Sanctuary (1964-1990), I poured a great deal of my life's energy into building membership and helping to purchase and protect
more ecologically valuable land adjacent to the Ridges, bringing the
total up to slightly more than 1,000 acres by 1990 when I finished my

work there. The famous Jens Jensen of The Clearing would have been extremely happy, for it was he who planted the goal for the Ridges to continually work toward acquiring at least 1,000 acres. These extended land purchases, based upon his past experiences and great wisdom, would be needed to protect the especially valuable front and newly developing ridges.

It was quite natural that my excitement and understanding of this world-famous ridge-swale formation continued to grow during the 27 years I worked diligently to educate people of all ages and build interest in this spectacular boreal forest geological and botanical gem.

Dave Thomas, realtor from northern Door County, invited me to fly with him over the northern Lake Michigan shores several years ago. He was intent upon introducing me to the incredibly extensive ridge-swale complexes — perhaps more than 50 to 100 consecutive water- and wind-formed ridges in one area that were quite clearly made by natural forces following the retreat from Wisconsin of the last glacier around 10,000 years ago.

Whenever a community, township, or county owns such a geological and botanical rarity, which invariably is also rich in animal life, the people should guard it very jealously. What innumerable recreational, research, and educational opportunities lie there.

It's easy to imagine the excitement that would have been exhibited by the Group of Seven, years ago upon being introduced to the forested ridge-swale area that lies south of the Sturgeon Bay Ship Canal, land that is owned by the city of Sturgeon Bay. You can easily understand the consternation and dismay of those people today who have come to understand the incredible ecological biodiversity of this area upon learning that much of it is being slated to be logged in the near future.

Imagine the huge disappointment of the long-time Sturgeon Bay High School biology teacher Carl Cochrane and his students upon hearing that such utter destruction had been brought about to the fragile wooded ridges within the Ship Canal woods where Carl has taken many of his classes to study and to learn in past years.

I have always been strongly convinced that nature does not exist for the convenience of man. Does all land have to show a monetary profit? Rare plants, a few declared to be state and federally threatened, grow in the woods along the Ship Canal. Among them are the moonwort fern, dwarf lake iris, dune thistle, dune goldenrod, fringed gentian, pink moccasin flower, three species of coralroot orchids and the ladies' tresses orchid. It would be next to impossible to estimate the huge monetary value of these woods and ridges to the learning of our young people as well as to the sheer enjoyment of the many people hiking there and enjoying nature at its finest.

These ridges are very fascinating botanically in that they lie north and south in their orientation, very similar to the famous ridge-swale complex existing at the Point Beach State Forest along the shore of Lake Michigan north of Two Rivers, Wisconsin. This botanical paradise is also much like those at the Jackson Harbor Ridges on Rock Island to the north of Washington Island in northern Door County. Both of these sites contain considerably higher and steeper ridges than those at the Ridges Sanctuary at Baileys Harbor. These run east and west, are much lower in elevation, and have a different microclimate.

Years ago my friend Sister Julia Van Denak of Holy Family College south of Manitowoc, Wisconsin wrote her Ph.D. thesis on the vegetation of the ridges and swales at Point Beach State Forest. Later, as a professor at the Holy Family College, she often hiked with me at the Ridges Sanctuary during my early years there, and we had long talks about the similarity and differences regarding the plant and animal life of the Point Beach and Baileys Harbor ridges. How exciting it would be to obtain a copy of Sister Julia's thesis and to compare the plants that she studied so thoroughly at Point Beach years ago with those existing today in the Sturgeon Bay Ship Canal ridges and swales.

The Sturgeon Bay Ship Canal woods is an area which, with proper management, can serve as a rich natural area helping people to recreate and to learn about nature for years to come. Conditions here are ideal for conducting meaningful research and for collecting valuable baseline data that will increase in value from year to year. Furthermore, this high-quality area of rich biodiversity would, in my estimation, easily qualify to become a new State Natural Area.

Dr. Fuller, one of the Group of Seven, the individual whom I visualize as the real "Father of the Ridges Sanctuary," came to thoroughly know the plants of our state as well as those from many other parts of the country and the world. When he was informed that the Baileys Harbor ridges were destined to be made into a campground in the mid-1930s he was furious. He lost little time in telling the Door County Park Commission something to the effect that if large cities in crowded Europe such as London or Berlin suddenly and magically were able to have the plant-rich ridges within their boundaries, they would pay millions of dollars for the privilege, and here you are going to destroy those at Baileys Harbor. The very same holds true today for the Canal woods and ridges.

Notes from a Fisherman/Singer/Songwriter
(Hibbards Creek Preserve)

by Mark Raddatz

Spring...the late seventies? I remember the way the cool, clean water rippled over the stones, toward the mouth of the creek. And further upstream, the configuration of logs that had randomly toppled over...storms, windfall, decay...rerouting the currents in the stream. It was springtime, and it was bordered with lush greenery, white birch, and the occasional wildflower. Beautiful.

The best fishing gear for Hibbards would be ultralight fishing tackle. Short rods — there's a lot of brush. Spinner and garden worms for bait. But wait a minute. I'm thinking of how it used to be, when the Department of Natural Resources (DNR) used to stock all the streams with beautifully speckled brook trout, much favored by fathers taking young kids fishing. The brookies were plentiful, easier to catch than the cagey, bigger steelhead. The brookies are smaller and make tastier table fare. You could catch your limit in no time and have a good meal.

Fishing Hibbard conjured images of Nick Adams in a Hemingway short story, exploring the stream with vivid descriptions...even the sandwiches he packed for the excursion, thinly sliced onion on buttered bread, seasoned with salt and pepper.

I miss those days. Some of my best fishing memories.

These days I don't catch much on Hibbard. You need more sophisticated, expensive gear and the patience of a saint, for you could fish the creek all day and still come home empty-handed.

*

Walking the creek, from County A westward, with my youngest son, Seth.

It is late October, late afternoon on a Sunday. Many of the leaves have fallen. We step over the soft, padded earth. Dead fall on both sides of the creek, which is now but shallow, isolated pools of water. Some are clear, some dark and murky which sometimes mimics my mood at this time of year. Too late for fishing — merely hiking now. and knowing winter will soon be coming. There's a chill in the air, after a light rain.

We stop, sit on a log and munch on a light afternoon meal we packed. For Seth, a carefully built (by him) variation of a Chicago hot dog, and for me, that thinly sliced onion and butter sandwich...from that Hemingway story.

Seth finds a couple of walking sticks and we continue our hike, sometimes gathering leaves of maple, birch, occasional elms. Overhead we hear the call of geese over Kangaroo Lake — the call of the wild.

Starting to sprinkle a little again. We stop and watch the myriad pools on the creek water created by the droplets of rain. We come to a man-made wooden bridge across the creek and decide to turn back. The rain keeps coming down.

*

Hibbards in spring, my favorite time of year for fishing. Everything starting to bloom. Life is beginning again. Fish are cruising the fast-moving waters, usually deeper this time of year, depending on the amount of winter snow, spring rains, and the overall level of Lake Michigan...in most recent years, receding...affecting the quality of sport fishing.

In years past, as I mentioned before, the fishing was superb back when the DNR was stocking brook trout. I spoke to a DNR man recently who said there wasn't much demand for that type of fishing. Bull! There's just not enough revenue in it for them.

In summer, the stream flow slows down a bit. But it's still surrounded by lush greenery and fun to hike. In fall, the trees bordering the stream are ablaze with color, and the climate is still pleasant enough to walk, take photographs, paint, or picnic. By winter, the creek is either dry or, depending on the lake level and speed of flow, iced over. Some spots may even be good for skating. And with all the leaves gone from the trees, there's a little more of a vista up- or downstream.

*

It's important to preserve Hibbards Creek for future generations to enjoy. More and more land in this county keeps getting lost to private ownership, wealthy corporations. It's as if poor to moderate-income folks somehow don't deserve to enjoy the natural beauty of their surroundings. There's an influx of the wealthy to naturally desirable areas. The property values rise and folks who have lived in these places all their lives can't afford to any more.

I remember walking Hibbards with an old school chum and someone rode up on a four-wheeler and said we couldn't be there because he had just purchased most of the land surrounding Hibbards immediately west of Highway 57.

It made me think of the seldom-sung line from Woody Guthrie's "This Land Is Your Land": one side of a sign said "No Trespassin', the other side, it didn't say nothin', that side was made for you and me."

So _ _ _ _ Mr. Four-wheeler. I'll take my kids and my friends and hike along any ol' stream. Like many other areas of this county, things have gone the way of that proverbial hellish handbasket, by now sporting some sort of offensive upscale designer label.

*

I've hiked or fished Hibbards from County A eastward past Highway 57 to the mouth, and westward from County A almost to the source. The color ranges from crystal clear to sandy to rusty-colored and almost blackish in spots, depending on the amount of sunlight and the composition of the creek bottom.

I've had some good adventures and memories by it and in it. I remember taking the kids there when they were younger to fish for small rainbows. At one point I snagged a lure in a low overhanging branch and had to strip down to my birthday suit to walk into the creek and unsnag it. Later we were walking back to the car and along the path we encountered a pretty girl who said "Hello" with a big grin on her face. I was thinking she may have spied me naked in the water. A bit embarassed, I said "Hello" back and kept walking.

Once my sons Austin and Seth and I were fishing by County A near the culvert, and stopped to have a picnic lunch of meatball sandwiches on homemade bread. In the same spot, later in the summer on a very hot day, Seth and I took a dip in the deep clear pool by the culvert.

One of my favorite memories of Hibbards is, every August I would play a gig down in Brussels at Julie's Sugar Mountain Farm Market. It was usually pretty hot that time of year, so on the way home, Susan and I would stop along 57 in Jacksonport and walk upstream a little ways, get naked, and sit among the tiny, darting crayfish in the cool, clear waters. She was pregnant with Seth then, and it was soothing for her to sit in the refreshing waters. The next year, on the way home we stopped there again, holding Seth in the cool water with us, just enjoying out surroundings. It was very private and very quiet, except for the sound of the trickling stream and the birds chirping — a real memorable experience.

*

If I were to scratch some words, some lines toward a song about Hibbards and all this...

In the Flowing Waters

In the flowing waters
we made love
amid the birds, fish, and trees,
We drank of each other,
tasted our dreams,
touched our hearts, explored our souls,
sang songs to our baby,
ate our lunch,
sipped our wine,
bathed our weary bodies,
washed away our sins,
taught our kids to fish, wade, swim, hike
and appreciate the outdoors,
practically in their own backyard.

This place in time was, is, ours, theirs,
everybody's to revel in and nurture
for our children's children. Always and evermore.

A truly beautiful and quiet haven
these flowing waters
we made ours,
without depriving others.

*

"This land is your land
This land is my land"
—Woody Guthrie

A Thin Place: The Gabert Family Farm
(Oak Road Wetland Preserve)
by Laurel Hauser

In the 7th century, St. Angus journeyed to the valley of Balquidder in the Scottish Highlands. Moved profoundly by its beauty, he described it as a "thin place," a place where heaven and earth almost touch.

In the Celtic tradition, thin places are the rare, quiet places that allow us to glimpse, for a moment, a world more timeless and enduring than our own. Their effect is profound and difficult to describe; the best we can say is that when we are fortunate enough to experience one, we are marked in some indelible way.

While wandering in search of someplace else quite a few years ago, I became temporarily lost and happened upon a thin place. I was a few miles inland from Carlsville crisscrossing unfamiliar country intersections when I turned onto a quiet road. I followed it for a short distance when it rounded a sharp bend and dipped low, and I found myself in a land transformed. A bayou-like lake, almost at road level, appeared out of nowhere on my right. Tall trees and a resounding chorus of amphibians and echoing bird calls rose out of the low-hanging mist. It was magical.

I didn't know it at the time, but I was on Oak Road. I stopped the car, transfixed. I felt that I had happened upon some secret and ephemeral place. I had the distinct impression that when this land and lake disappeared from my rear-view window, it would disappear altogether. I eventually found my destination that day and didn't think again about the magical place until I came upon it again years later. Even though it was not a misty spring day and the seasonal "lake" was gone, I immediately knew that this was the "thin place" I had experienced all those years before.

Thin places are not necessarily exotic or dramatic or even remote, and Oak Road is none of these. It is not a wild place. Nestled among surrounding farms and plowed rolling hills, it is pastoral. Situated in a valley, it has a safe, tucked-in quality. The roads around it gently curve and dip and bend. They are less stridently utilitarian than most and defy the Jeffersonian ideal of square corners. They give the impression that they were decided upon by herds of cows rather than men. If the acres around Oak Road could speak, they might say, "with some hard work, life here is almost guaranteed to be good. Nothing here is apt to go fundamentally wrong." Those of us who grew up watching the Waltons might almost hear the familiar "goodnight, John Boy" echo from a nearby farmhouse on a warm summer evening.

Since 1910, the story of Oak Road has been tied to the story of the Gabert family. In that year, August and Lillian Gabert declared that "the city" was no place to raise a family. They packed up their 12 children and left the thriving metropolis of Sturgeon Bay (population just over 3,000) for life in the country. They purchased 80 acres and immediately began to build the smal white frame house that still stands today. While building it, they lived in a log home already on the property. In the winter, the wind blew snow through the walls and their incentive to finish their new home was great. Every family member was conscripted, including one of the youngest, Tilden, age 5. According to Tilden's daughter, Nancy Gabert Mueller, her father had clear memories of helping build the house he would live in for the next nine decades.

Tilden Gabert grew up surrounded by families similar to his own. Trent Gabert, Tilden's son and Nancy's brother, recounts that most of the families on the surrounding farms had 11 to 15 children. "The Neimeyers down the road raised 11 children in a two-bedroom house. As one kid got older, he was moved out to the barn to sleep in the haymow and a younger kid got his bed. There was a lot of interaction between the neighboring families, and neighbors were very important to my parents. That is one of the largest changes I see from my parents' generation to ours."

Early plat books of the Oak Road area show a virtually unchanging patchwork quilt of family names on 40-acre plots—the Kuehns, Simonars, Neimeyers, Orthobers, Spittlemeisters and Geitners. A piece of land was referred to as the Mosgaller farm or the Schwichtenberg farm and was likely to be so for as long as anyone cared to guess. Life, including courtship, happened on a very local level and Tilden met Bernice, a Carlsville Schuster, at the Carlsville School Box Social. Like other young ladies of the area, Bernice decorated a box filled with her best cooking and baking. The decorated boxes were auctioned off, with the high bidder winning the box and the privilege of enjoying its contents with the young lady who made it. Tilden and Bernice ate a picnic lunch together that day and were eventually married. As often happened, Bernice moved to the Gabert homestead. She and Tilden shared it with Tilden's mother and brother until their third baby was born. By that time, the Gaberts had purchased two additional 40's, and Tilden's mother and brother moved to a farmhouse just across the road.

For the next half a century, Tilden and Bernice raised their three children, tended 11 acres of orchard trees, milked 25 to 30 cows morning and night, planted and harvested a large garden, grew rows and rows of raspberries, and plowed and worked 160 acres of land. Tilden also acted as Egg Harbor town chairman for many years, and Bernice wrote the Sunny Point column for the *Advocate*.

Tilden and Bernice's children, Nancy, Augie, and Trent, grew up with strong connections to the land. Nancy remembers the marsh playing a big part in their childhood. "Folks called our farm 'Frog Town,'. In the spring when the marsh was full, it was so loud you could barely sleep." Trent adds, "We had an old rowboat we would row out to an island on the east end of the marsh. My brother and I would take lunch out and cut branches and build tree houses. It was our island, away from everything. Other times we would just wade through the water catching frogs and enjoying the feeling of the mud from the bottom oozing up between our toes. If there was enough water in the winter, we'd ice skate on the marsh."

Life, even life on the farm, changed quickly in the mid-1900s. Trent recalls being taken to school on bad weather days in his father's six-passenger, enclosed one-horse sleigh. "Education was important and weather wasn't supposed to interfere with going to school!" Later, a pick-up truck would replace the sleigh and still later a school bus replaced the truck. In good weather, "we walked home. It was actually fun, especially in the fall when the Spittlemeisters' apples and plums were ripe!"

While good, life on the farm was also hard. "We all worked in one way or another," Trent explains. "This really became full-time when my uncle was killed in an automobile accident and my dad had to run both farms. We had 5 a.m. milkings and all the other farm work. The greatest invention during my life was electricity. When it came to the farm, wow— lights, hot water, milking machines!"

Augie recalls the especially taxing cherry harvests, an annual Door County event. "I can recall the smudge pots on cold nights to reduce the danger of frost. During the harvest season, my dad would spend many hours waiting in line with our truck of cherries at Reynolds Brothers canning factory. The harvest was very hectic for our whole family as we milked the cows, picked up people to pick the cherries, helped with the picking, took the pickers home and kept track of the punched cards for each worker. My dad was an expert pruner and he helped many of the other orchard growers with that job."

Both 8th grade graduates, Tilden and Bernice insisted that their children receive educations. "Our parents often talked about wanting us to have a better and perhaps easier life than farming. Dairy farming is really hard work seven days a week. Thus, they stressed education. Several of our uncles were in law and medicine and they were the models our parents thought of. So, while we enjoyed the farm, there was never discussion of any of us taking it over."

Nancy, Augie, and Trent were all educated (one B.A. and two Ph.D.s), and all did leave the farm. *Their* children are now spread coast to coast and across oceans, from Singapore to Las Vegas to Washington D.C. and Alaska.

The Gabert story echoes many others in Door County and across the country. In Richard Louv's *Last Child in the Woods*, he states that in 1993, "the *Washington Post* reported in 'a symbol of massive national transformation,' the federal government dropped its long-standing annual survey of farm residents. Farm population had dwindled so much — from 40 percent of U.S. households in 1900 to just 1.9 percent in 1990 — that the farm resident survey was irrelevant." He goes on to say that "this new, symbolic demarcation line suggests that baby boomers — Americans born between 1946 and 1964 — may constitute the last generation of Americans to share an intimate, familial attachment to the land and water."

Trent reports that his own children "enjoy Door County and the farm area, but they never experienced real work on the farm. When we visited it was a vacation. They never *had* to work on the farm, thus their idea of farming is the same as any city person's today."

Tilden and Bernice saw that things were changing. Nancy recounts that when her father retired at age 65 and stopped milking cows, he talked about selling his farm. "He always returned to the fact that they were not 'city people.' Also, they worried about what would happen to the property if they sold it. It bothered them to no end all the development and condominiums. It was always a topic of conversation. Development rubbed all of us the wrong way. Mom died in 1994 and Dad continued to live on the farm. He felt very responsible about its future. Even if he wasn't going to be here, he felt responsibility toward the neighbors. During the last few years when Dad was in the hospital nursing home, we'd bring him back here to visit. He maintained relations with the neighbors and they would often ask what was to become of the land."

Tilden passed away in 2003 at the age of 98. The house he helped build still stands; his name is still faintly visible on the old mailbox. When the Gabert children began to contemplate the farm's future, a few events converged, and in Nancy's words, "the right thing happened."

Not long ago, Mary Standish, a Door County Land Trust board member, happened as I had upon Oak Road. Whether she would describe it as a "thin place" or not, she knew it was something special. At her urging, Terrie Cooper, the Land Trust's land program director, placed a tentative phone call to Trent Gabert to inquire about possibly purchasing this special place. She vividly recalls the conversation. "I was very nervous. At the time, the Land Trust had no money for such an ambitious project and no idea where we would get the funding. All we had was the idea and Mary's infectious passion."

Trent spoke to his siblings, who were intrigued. Terrie and Dan Burke, the Land Trust's executive director, went to work. Through some creative negotiations with the Knowles-Nelson State Stewardship Fund, a grant from the U.S. Fish and Wildlife Service's Natural Resource Damage Assessment program, support from some of the Gabert neighbors and other Land Trust members, all of the necessary funds were raised. On January 12, 2006, the Gabert land became permanently protected as the Oak Road Preserve.

"By preserving this land, we are honoring our parents' years of hard work. We are creating their memorial. Our parents were very generous people. They gave armloads of garden produce to anyone who stopped by. They loved this land, the springtime waters, the waterfowl, and the frogs. They would appreciate that it will be preserved for others to learn from and enjoy. We want to give to others what our parents gave to us. This is the right thing to do."

The Gabert story is a hopeful one at a time when farms are disappearing at an alarming rate. Cut up and divided, they become one- or five-acre lots that leave little room for wildlife or quiet wandering or childhood adventures. They leave little room for "thin places." In a world thick with human constructs, to experience a thin place is a memorable and sacred occurrence. Luckily for all of us, one of Door County's thin places, the Oak Road Wetland Preserve, will be around for a long, long time.

Uprooted
by Charlotte Johnston

In a boreal forest near Lake Michigan's shoreline,
        rough coral and smooth beach stones
rest together on a high ridge where once
                an inland sea washed its hair.
Lead-heavy cushions of granite
        left by the glacier's Green Bay lobe
mark a precarious path over
        roots and narrow channels where seven
                intruders explore
                        an eerie wilderness.
With lateral roots exposed
        and brittle branches reaching out,
storm-toppled cedars
                lie in the arms of brothers
                        blocking the trail.
Inhaling its musky dampness…
            hearing no bird songs
                    nor animal stirrings…
seven uprooted travelers stumble on for hours
weaving through thick stands
            of balsam and birch,
                thimbleberry and bracken fern
                            until at last…
    the weary pilgrims emerge,
            rescued by the road and open light.

Old Stage Road Scenic Corridor
by Norbert Blei

Road Notes

After thirty years of living in Door, I can drive Old Stage Road in the dark with my eyes closed. I've known it through blizzard and ice, hard rain, heat wave, howling wind, morning, noon, night and, ah, the magic of fog. A road for all seasons.

Winter Note: *Snow has been falling all night. Mine are the first tracks in the thinning dark, lifting now in the east, over the lake. Headlights probe the emptiness, seeking direction down Old Stage...the road at this hour before daylight...the trees, the fences, the fields...everything transformed. Glowing with an inner light.*

Not one of my favorite back roads. Not by a long shot. Those I keep to myself for when I need them. But not a road without some local history and a touch of old, back road, Wisconsin rural character— what remains. Which is why I find myself on Old Stage again (in mind, in place) contemplating, 'the road' from all manner of measure and perspective, working through memories and notes, looking for a way to say what must be said about 'the way' of country roads, given a county so filled with nature's wonder yet so mindful of tourism for survival, so threatened by over development and the persistence of change.

Remember...Robert Frost's poem, "The Road Not Taken":

*"I took the one less traveled by,
And that has made all the difference"*

~

Driving Old Stage, or any other side road, back road, remaining dirt road through Door, ostensibly "to get somewhere" though, truth

to tell, a desire to lose time, kill time, *be* on the road, destination nowhere, is the real road trip. To enter the landscape, find and feel the
quiet again, drift down roadways through woods, fields, and farms,
cruise *under* the speed limit, know one's place without thinking, deep
in the nature of Nature, home free—only to be suddenly drawn short
these days—foot-on-the-brake...'Oh, no!' you hear yourself say. Eyes
focused on the intruder in plain sight: Bulldozer At Work. Grind.
Crunch. Screech. Cold steel mauling earth, stone, bush...cat-tracks
turning, crashing helter-skelter through old trees, a mechanical dance
macabre, triggering anger impossible to describe—or justify: "WHAT
THE HELL ARE YOU DOING WITH MY _____?" My? My road?
My view? My land? My place? My county?"

Making its way, of course. Making inroads for another new resident thrilled to be building a second or third vacation home—this one
in Door County. It's the ubiquitous invasion of the McMansions, the
American Dream gone nightmare. Humongous habitats with stone-
pillared entrances and wrought iron gates (cute names like Innesfree
glowing on bronze plaques). Porticos (*portes cochère*)—formal front
entrances with high-hanging chandeliers over fussy front doors, waiting for the BMW's, Benz's, Rolls Royce's to begin rolling in, deposit-
ing dinner guests. Country castles of faux Greek columns, dead brick,
rooflines ala' grandiose (turrets et. al), gables galore, dozens of dor-
mers, windows everywhere (small, medium, large, extra large) looking out toward the plebeians passing by (hopefully awestruck), while
the last farmer, staring straight ahead, put-puts along on a groaning
tractor, pulling a wagonload of sweet manure, giving no mind to
McMansion majesty, figuring behind all those windows lay a heap of
nothing going on anyways.

Though something is. The end of something for sure.

Every back road in Door County is an Old Stage Road in jeopardy
of its natural pathway through landscape and history. The character it
lends to the total aura of one of the most beautiful counties in the
Midwest. A county presently bound for a new history of no matter. A
history of more acreage to be worked over in ways that can only di-
minish and destroy what drew us all here in the first place. Another
back road hell-bent to go McMansion, eating up the view, renovating
the rural landscape. Rooting out woods. Smoothing the earth. Land-
scaping it down, up, sideways to the hired landscaper's desire. Black-
topping it. Beating down whatever of the wild that's in the way...that
doesn't echo the occupant's social status, the image of where "they're
from" be it city, lakeside condo, wealthy suburb, or gated community.

"Tara" transplanted North. Big Foot (print) stomped hard upon
native hardscrabble. Conspicuous consumption come home to strut in

County Door, where the living is easy (for some), all the landscape's
for sale, and the mission is to modify, occupy, replace. To change forever the sense of "road rural"...the white farmhouses, the deep
woods, the serene farm fields which give us pause, address a certain
peace in openness all around us, both sides of the road, as far as the
eye could see, to sustain our sense of being with the land.

What are you doing with my...?

All of which I take as a personal affront. Though none of this is
mine (or ours). Yet in a larger sense, it all belongs to us. All that I view
and speaks to me on both sides of Old Stage Road (or any old Door
County back road)...the trees, the fields, the farms, the flowers in the
ditches along the roadside...how the seasons work their wonder upon
the bountiful emptiness of this holy rural space, always surprising us
with yet something else we missed before: a wild apple tree, a deer-
stand stuck high in a tree, the field of blue forget-me-nots we keep
forgetting each new spring. All this and more belong to us. With the
understanding, unwritten, unexpressed, that it's ours to acknowledge
and protect.

Preservation or profit? It comes down to that.

You gnaw on this for a moment, while the bulldozer in your rear
view mirror, digs a little deeper into your consciousness, only to leave
you with that contentious word 'progress' (so beloved by chambers of
commerce, local newspaper editors, merchants, realtors, developers)
which burns like a fever within because you know in your heart
'progress' means business—and can't be stopped. All this 'scenery'
you are taking in for the good of the soul is destined to be turned
under, tamed, rendered into a nature of suburban aesthetics bordering
on the grotesque—according to plan. Controllable. Predictable. Dead.
You mull on that longer that you like and maybe pull to the side
of the road, under the shade of a large white birch, or alongside a
stand of pine, roll down the driver's window, take a deep breath...
recalling the scent of wild clover in June. This vista, that field
stretched to the horizon, the patterns of that stone fence under snow
cover, come February. The way it used to be: Door County's pine-
scented, lake-washed fresh air...where visitors came in summer
because the land was naturally conditioned by cool, lake air.
You lean into the rough bark of a towering maple, or follow that
old stone fence line for a bit, alive in the quiet that takes hold, the
consuming emptiness of the fields. Thankful for what remains rural,

as true to itself as a weathered barn, a flowering lilac bush all agog against an old white farmhouse, or a hanging stone left over from glacier days, worn smooth and creamy, wrapped in rusty barbed wire, weighing down a ravaged cedar fence post leaning closer and closer to earth...its last stand. Its purpose—crops, pasture, horses, cattle—now history.

But the image of the bulldozer (crawler, caterpillar, tractor) invading the earth with ferocious upheavals, continues to invade the mind's eye. If you read Steinbeck at an impressionable age, if you journeyed down *that* road west with the Joad family in *The Grapes Of Wrath*, you can never quite shake the image of the tractor Steinbeck described in his time, the 1930s, which speaks to our time too. (As I write, a dozer cutting a new access-road into a field half-way down Old Stage):

The tractors came over the roads and into the fields, great crawlers moving like insects, having the incredible strength of insects...Snub-nosed monsters, raising the dust and sticking their snouts into it...through fences, through dooryards ...The man sitting in the seat did not look like a man: gloved, goggled, rubber dust mask over nose and mouth, he was part of the monster, a robot in the seat...The driver could not control it—straight across country it went, cutting through a dozen farms...because the monster that built the tractor, the monster that sent the tractor out, had somehow got into the driver's hands, into his brain and muscle, had goggled him and muzzled him—goggled his mind, muzzled his speech, goggled his perception, muzzled his protest. He could not see the land as it was, he could not smell the land as it smelled; his feet did not stomp the clods or feel the warmth and power of the earth...He loved the land no more than the bank loved the land.

~

Roads change. Broaden. Connect. Turn upon themselves. Grow into highways, expressways. Become numbers. Lose purpose and direction. Become unused. Neglected. Abandoned. Disappear—back to earth, weeds breaking through asphalt and concrete cracks. Become nameless. Lose character, serenity—their original mission into the interior. Dead end.

~

Old Stage Road is considered by some a 'corridor'—an urban connotation out of place around here. To me, any road off the main highway in a rural setting is a back road. The farther it takes me away from the main road, the better. I don't even care what it's called. Just take me somewhere real, fresh and different. Expand my horizons. Surprise me. Comfort me. Even lose me. Old Stage, as far as I'm concerned, is still a back road. Possibly a passageway. Though locals and some visitors consider it at times, a bypass.

Historically (since the heavy tourism of the 1980s to the present— from July 4th 'till Fall Fest in October) Old Stage has become just that: a bypass (going north or south) around the daily downtown traffic of Sister Bay during the high season when cars, trucks, campers, biker-packs, and tourist busses lumber along the main drag, slow down to check the goats on top of Al Johnson's grass roof, start up and slow down again to gaze at a sunset over the harbor...stop, start, stop, start... and you either go with that timeless stop-&-go-flow, or look for a way out. And that way out is Old Stage, running almost parallel, some distance away, east of the main drag, which you can either pick up, eventually or in desperation, (should you find yourself caught in the midst of a goat-gawk procession) on almost any side road, jutting east off the main drag through Sister Bay.

Your first best shot, coming down the Sister Bay hill (junction of Highway 57 and 42), is Maple Road/County ZZ: turn right at the bottom of the hill (the corner of the Sister Bay Bowl and Jungwirth Hardware). After that, in order and all right turns, it's: Scandia Road; Hill Road; Waters End Road; and further down the highway, Wildwood, Green, and Highview Roads. Which by then just about puts you near the end of Old Stage (north) as it meets Highway 57—Ellison Bay just ahead. The whole stretch, from where Old Stage begins (or ends), south of Sister Bay, till it joins Highway 42 outside Ellison Bay, a total of 7.2 miles, and just under ten minutes of driving time.

But if you're new to the county, headed north out of Baileys Harbor on Highway 57, watch for the Old Stage Rd. sign on your right (about a mile and a half south of Sister Bay—"as the crow flies" as they used to say) and turn right if you like to explore life beyond the main highways, or avoid all the summer chaos just ahead.

Consider this a practical road guide for the moment. But stay with me for the real directions that matter. A guide to the interior.

~

There are always books in my desk as I write: preparation, consultation, inspiration. I open an old copy of *The Narrow Road To The Deep North*, by Matsuo Basho (1644-94). Inspiration—for road travel. I turn to the final page and reflect on the postscript to Basho's journey by the monk, Soryu in 1694:

In this little book of travel is included everything under the sky —not only that which is hoary and dry but also that which is young and colorful, not only that which is strong and imposing but also that which is feeble and ephemeral. As we turn every corner of the Narrow Road to the Deep North, we sometimes stand up unawares to applaud and we sometimes fall flat to resist the agonizing pains we feel in the depths of our hearts. There are also times when we feel like taking to the road ourselves, seizing the raincoat lying nearby, or times when we feel like sitting down till our legs take root, enjoying the scene we picture before our eyes...

The real journey is the journey within. The true road gets us there without our knowing. We do not take the road; the road takes us to where we *have* to go.

All roads lead to philosophy, if we read the un-posted signs.

~

I proceed along Old Stage this way for the moment, finding my bearings on a county road older than anyone traveling it these days.

I even consider it before it became Old Stage Road. Who cut into the virgin timber and fields? Who decided: "Let's go this way?"

Origins. History. Settling new territory. How it all started with animal paths, no doubt. The path, the trail, the dirt road, the main road, the paved road, the highway. Those inner and outer connections to where we find ourselves, in motion, headed somewhere.

Travelers on Old Stage these days rarely ponder the road's name other than to perhaps picture a stage coach from some western movie. Though that was not the type of stage that once rattled down this old road. Just what *did* a Door County stage looked like in those days, late 1800 to early 1900s ?

I'll look into that—a little further down the road.

Early pioneer trail conditions? Bumpy, rocky, rutted no doubt. Up and down. Occasionally level. Mud and water holes. Good places to sink a wagon wheel axle-deep and get stuck. Maybe tip the whole damn shebang over. A hard ride for sure. Bone crushing. Distance to be traveled, to be felt every inch of the way, men, women, and children sitting/bobbing on wooden benches, under some kind of covering to protect them from the unpredictable weather of a northeastern peninsula, jutting into Lake Michigan. A seasonal assortment of cold, wind, rain, fog, snow, blizzard, sleet, spring breezes, a touch of summer heat and lightning storms. Pre-global warming, for sure.

There were no bridges to cross on this route. No rivers to ford. Though locals, like Ron Beno, local history buff and ace auto mechanic of Baileys Harbor, will tell you of tales and times in wicked winter storms when horse drawn sleighs rode drifts high up and over stone fences. No road in sight. And how, in one instance he recalls, the body of an old farm woman was left in the machine shed from January to March, when they could finally get her to the undertaker in Sister Bay.

You think about all this sometime—the lay of the land along Old Stage, along any rural back road. As it was then. As it is now.

~

As it is now...once you made that turn off Highway 57 onto Old Stage (driving more or less east), it's all pretty much what you would expect, depending on your own history of this place, what and who you know and remember...how long you have lived or vacationed here. Some solid lines of cedar on both sides of the road, a scattering of nice homes and manicured lawns, open fields and more trees. Pretty much basic cool, calm countryside, slowly infiltrated by newcomers, new homes spaced accordingly, a little more acreage squared off, populated, lost to what was once the great sweep of fields and working farms. You can almost see and feel that yet, along parts of this stretch, though everything's changing.

On the northeast corner of Old Stage and Orchard sits a large new house, some distance back, where once the old white falling-down farm house, weathered barn, and ramshackle outbuildings of Henry Lang, a local Mr. Fix-it, stood. All the Mr. Fix-its (who could fix anything, never knew what to charge for their efforts, so pretty much fixed it for nothing plus a promise) are gone now. And Henry on Old Stage was one of the best, when it came to small appliances. I couldn't begin to describe the inside of his shop. If I did, you wouldn't believe it.

Further down, along this stretch of Old Stage, if you're lucky, you might see horses off to your right, always a magnificent sight to behold while road wandering. A comfort and throwback to what once defined this piece of the rural countryside. Silos. Log Buildings. Split-rail fences. Well-kept or rusty rural mail boxes with up or down red flags, to keep the communication going. ("Rural Delivery"—how much longer before that's gone?)

The Ingwersen house/studio/compound (James Ingwersen, one of the county most illustrious artists) slips into view next, catching and keeping the traveler's eye with its plain, natural sense of place. It *is* where it belongs. Speaks the language of place. A careful blending of old and new by way of a house, barn and outbuildings...logs, weathered wood...'time' the true conditioner... all rendered whole, authentic in the landscape. The antithesis of McMansion macabre.

Fields on both sides come in after this, and a farm deep in the interior, far back from the road. Old Stage takes a slow but definite turn then, almost due north. The longest stretch, straight ahead. A very small farm crops up on the left with a sign, in summer, FOR SALE HAY. A particularly beautiful stretch in autumn, when all the woods do their magic act of green to yellow, red, orange and gold. And all the burnished fields lie down, even lower, waiting for their white winter blanket.

This is a stretch of Old Stage in transition. The old and the new. A brave attempt to redefine itself, as here and there industrial parks (around the corner, in the area of County ZZ and Old Stage) vie with a renovated old schoolhouse (with haunted basketball court), storage sheds, and the Going Garbage Company. A busy spot. But all this passes from view rather quickly, and the rural resonates once again in stone fences, large maples and pine, a scattering of dwellings. Even the persistence of what might yet pass for prairie.

Back roads like this either address your powers of concentration, objects in the landscape that speak of a more meaningful life, or lull you into a monotonous, meditative state of peaceful abandon, memories of wind through the open window, the smell of hay, patches of orange tiger lilies wild in the roadside ditch, trumpeting the sun… everything turning as the wheels of the car continue to turn, carrying you further and further into what lies ahead or just being here, in place, in a kind of standstill motion.

Past that great old weather-beaten barn with white stars (Jody Littler's place) where in fall you'll see a large APPLES sign on the road, near the corner of Old Stage and Scandia Rd. The kind of barn that occasionally draws an artist to pull over and park, set up shop, and try his hand at revealing whatever tale the barn has to tell. A painting that may someday hang in a home far away from here, where someone may feel the need to draw upon such sustenance, found only on a rural back road.

Past the northeast corner of Hill Rd. and Old Stage where the Sister Bay Moravian Church makes its plain but perfect presence known and felt, deep in the quiet countryside. No air of big city Mega-McChurch arrogance about it. Only the essentials: a quiet space to worship; a small parsonage; a graveyard with its own history of parishioners. Everything pretty much in order. God at home in the countryside. The door is always open.

Past a small white farm house on the corner of Waters End Road with peaceful front porch, weathered out-buildings, a lush home garden, wooden swing, and beautiful shade trees …a classic house of its kind that speaks time present and time past, totally in touch with its natural surroundings. You glance at this setting and immediately feel a quiet come over you.

Past Wildwood Road, and the last working farm on Old Stage, Steve Kalms' place with the tree-shaded house, big red barn, pickup truck, and open fields filled with hay wagons. Another reminder 'the way it used to be,' how an agrarian culture shaped our view from the road: barbed wire fences, tractors, plows, combines, manure spreaders, silos, granaries, milk houses, haylofts, windmills and the peace of pastures. Horses, hogs, farm dogs and cats, cattle, sheep and cows. A time when dairy farms once ruled in Door, but today are fading fast from the scene.

Now near the end of the Old Stage run...a momentary pause in praise of an orchard-man (Dale Seaquist, and family) and a new orchard of young cherry trees, recently planted within view of the road. Nothing like the sight and memory of white blossoms and red ripe cherries hanging from the trees. Such faith in these times, this place...when land is more marketable than orchards and cherry crops.

And just across the road from this, yet another sign of the times, a new 'orchard' of another kind looming over the landscape, more indicative of the high-tech age we live in...blinking and humming, day and night. *Oh brave new world.* A field, a thin forest of terrestrial towers at the highest point on the peninsula (this far north) disseminating voices from everywhere and information. Cell phones in paradise. Technology, come home to roost along the road where once a stage coach rambled, bringing its own kind of old news.

How could the old stage driver ever imagine this?

~

But the past refuses to remain silent, begs to be heard, buried though it may be in so many faded images and layers of time along the road.

The trail comes to mind again. The way it was. Rocky, muddy, unforgiving. Logs thrown down in the low wet spots for traction. One or two horses pulling something the size and shape of a wagon... enclosed...people sitting somehow inside...on their way, further up the peninsula or headed back down again to Sturgeon Bay.

What *did* they look like, those old stage coaches?

There's not a lot of county stage coach history to be found...or old stage coaches, for that matter. You start asking around, and anyone who remembers something, remembers someone else who might remember more, but usually doesn't. A lot of dead ends. No drivers left. No old stage coach to be found..

Ron Beno in Baileys Harbor recalls a friend, an old stage driver by
the name of Harold ("Cowboy') Anderson, a tall drink of water who
always wore a cowboy hat and boots, who used to hang around Ron's
garage and had a lot of stories about driving the stage. Anderson
loved horses, began driving the stage in the early 1900s, around the
age of twelve. "Old Stage Road," Ron says," was probably an old
Indian trail," years before Cowboy Anderson drove a stage down it.

Bud Kalms, in Liberty Grove, says that his grandfather, Louis
Koessl, drove a local stage coach, around 1917 to 1925. Bud thinks that
the coach probably looked "something like an enclosed wagon."

Finally, I call upon my friend, the artist Charles (Chick) Peterson
in Ephraim, for his view of those times. No one has painted this
county more (water, land, people) and with more precision and passion, than Chick, who holds in his mind, heart, hands, an incredible
history of old Door which he has spent a good part of his lifetime
studying, rendering into art, at times "ghosting" images in the composition: old schooners and boats, fishermen, farms, farm machinery,
farmhouses, men, women and children at work, celebrations, auc-
tions, the faces of old pioneers, shops, roads, churches, schoolhouses,
barns, outbuildings...the fields, the bluffs, the landscape in all seasons, in all kinds of weather—above all, the poetry of water, which so
defines this place.

There are people these days who seek out a Peterson painting to
know and feel exactly how things once were. Authenticity, and admi-
rable trait.

What did an old stage coach look like? I ask him. He describes it
as kind of a box wagon, not as long as a hay wagon. Weathered wood,
not painted. An opening in the front with a bench across where the
driver held on to two horses (probably)...with a bench down either
side for the passengers.

I tell him what I know about Old Stage, the coaches, the stories
I've head about one old driver, Harold Anderson. I tell him about my
favorite Chekhov story, "Grief" and the coach driver in old Russia
who lost a son and how no one would listen to his story, and how at
the end of the day's work shared his grief in the barn with his horse,
the only one who would listen.

Had he ever seen an old coach? Yes, he says. He received a call
once from a farmer around Koepsel's (Sister Bay), who had something
in the barn he wanted to show him. It was an old stage coach.

Did he photograph it? No, but he sketched it.

A few days later Chick calls, tells me to stop by...he's found the
sketch. And a slide of a painting he once did, turning the stage into a
delivery wagon.

A few days after that, he calls again. He's just finished a painting he wants me to see.

It's all there: the stage, the barn, the weather, the ghost of the old driver, stopped in time

This is where the road ends: the past in our presence. To honor and preserve.

A Lesson in the Woods
The Richter Community Forest
by Gloria Small

When the ferry leaves the Northport dock and crosses the stretch of water that connects Green Bay with Lake Michigan known as "Death's Door," Washington Island is visible in the distance. Washington Island is known as the "Crown of Door County," as it sits on the map above the slender Door Peninsula that juts into Lake Michigan.

Trees are noticed first, varying shades of green blending into a forest pallette. Rocky beaches and staggered bluffs accent the trees. Deep green hemlocks tower above the maple, oak, birch, beech, and aspen. Cedars lean toward the shining water, roots grasping for support in the layered rock. Waterfront houses peer from between the trees.

As the ferry lands in Detroit Harbor, the car drives off on a blacktop dock owned by the Washington Island Ferry Line, with shops scattered on either side. Beyond this, the visitor gets his first glimpse of an island treasure, the Richter Community Forest.

The Richter Community Forest stretches north and east, following the gentle curves of Green Bay Road. Homes are found on the shore to the west of the forest. The Nature Trail, dedicated to Mary Richter, adjoins on the east and is accessible from Lobdell Point Road, as the road winds its way from the ferry dock to town.

From the beginning Washington Island has connected man and nature. The Potawatomi revered the land and sought harmony with it. The first explorer to set foot here, a Frenchman, Jean Nicolet in 1634, was looking for a waterway to the west. But the first true settlers were allowed to own land in this "Indian Territory" after the federal government bought the land in 1831 and it became the "Wisconsin Territory." Although Washington Island is known as the first Icelandic settlement in America, the first to come to the island were the Irish, not the Icelanders. The influx of immigrants brought change to the land, which began to disrupt that harmony with the land that had existed for centuries.

The early settlers of Washington Island looked to the water and to the land to survive. In 1850, 169 people called this newly organized town their home. Fishermen dropped nets and hauled in the day's catch. Farmers cut trees to clear the land, collected rocks from the soil, and piled them in stone fences visible even today as one travels the island.

But it was the trees themselves that provided the livelihood for so many. Logging was a big business in the late 1800s. Acres of land were clear-cut, and logs were hauled to the Freyburg Bros. mill in West Harbor for processing, or to other smaller mills scattered throughout the island. Steamers burned cordwood and carried the forest material to distant cities. Trees became telegraph poles and fence posts. The stately sugar maples and American beech were cut as firewood for heating buildings in the growing cities on Lake Michigan. White cedar was valuable as an excellent building material that resisted rotting. Oak, white pine, and maple trees became flooring, furniture, and homes. Men trying to survive in this remote place were changing the island, once covered with diversified forests.

A company from off the island has harvested the forest, now known as the Richter Community Forest, commercially three times since the 1970s. Each time trees were cut and piled on flatbed semis, transported by ferry, and hauled to mills in other parts of the state, with treetops left behind.

The process of reseeding and growth has rebuilt the forest though some of its diversification has been lost. Sugar maples, beech, and basswood are found throughout the forest. White birch and red oak are seen mostly in the northern section. Deer, which are plentiful on the island, select maple and oak shoots as food and stay away from young beech saplings, which are perhaps less tasty. As a result, there are areas in this forest now comprised mainly of beech trees. Little re-generation exists in the southern part of the property, where hemlock and cedar are most abundant. When the balance of nature is lost, it is difficult to reestablish.

In 2000 a Forest Stewardship Council-Certified forester came to Washington Island to install a floor in a home from flooring that had been produced by a timber co-op on the other side of the state. Timber co-ops are set up to produce environmentally friendly timber and to "add value" to the timber, so that landowners can profit from the sale of local products such as flooring, building materials, and wooden art pieces instead of selling timber solely for firewood, pulp, or lumber to be hauled away for processing.

A group of islanders met with the forester to learn more about his work. Soon they began to envision the possibilities of a managed forest for the island and a local timber co-op. Arni Richter, owner of the

Washington Island Ferry Line, was part of that core group.

In 2002 Arni, a generous man with strong Icelandic roots, donated his 160-acre forest to the Door County Land Trust, with a detailed document as to what he wanted to see happen there. A Forest Stewardship Council Certified Management Plan, the highest standard for forest management, was included in perpetuity along with the development protection of the land. He designated a five-acre plot for buildings for a timber co-op processing site and/or demonstration site for educational purposes. Because of his deep feelings for the island, its families, and the people who visit, Arni was committed to protecting this beautiful forest for recreational use, including hunting. He wanted to provide future jobs for islanders in selective tree harvesting and adding value to that forest product through local processing. He wanted a place for educational opportunities related to forest management.

The forest was appropriately named the Richter Community Forest, after Arni and his late wife Mary, who were both born on the island and lived their entire lives here. This donation of land protects one of the largest undeveloped properties on Washington Island, and gives the community an outdoor living classroom where people of all ages will be gathering for generations to come.

Dan Burke, the executive director of the Door County Land Trust, recognized the donation with these words, "Generosity, vision, and leadership is what it takes to successfully complete a project of this magnitude, and Mr. Richter definitely possesses all three."

The Richter Forest may become a model for other island forests.

Forest management principles will be followed for future harvesting of mature trees. Selection for cutting will be based on the needs of the forest. A healthy forest must have diversity in the age of the trees and in the species that comprise it. The Washington Island Family Forest Project, an alliance of the Wisconsin Family Forest, is closely tied to the Richter Forest. This organization's purpose is to connect communities to the land through sustainable forestry. It sponsors programs to educate the public and bring awareness of the forest. One program of special interest was a demonstration by horse logger Tim Carroll, who combines Old World skills with new-age technology and uses a horse team instead of a log skidder to haul the cut logs from the woods.

The Washington Island School is involved in the forest, too. Every class from the kindergarten through eighth grade visits the forest and nature trail. Each time I accompany students to this forest, the words of environmentalist Rachel Carson run through my mind:

"If a child is to keep alive his inborn sense of wonder without any such gift from the fairies, he needs the companionship of at least one adult who can share it, rediscovering with him the joy, excitement, and mystery of the world we live in."

Students hurry in eagerness down the path of wood chips into the forest as if the prize is at the end. They are too young to realize that the prize encompasses them. I need to remind them to "Stop! Listen! Look!" We stop to find something to share, and within a minute gleeful shouts are heard as a whole new world, the tiny forest animal community, is discovered. There are insects that scatter as a rock is turned, a salamander that is captured as he scurries out of wet leaves, and a spider in the center of a web stretched between low greenery. We form a circle and share our discoveries of worms, insects, and small creatures confined for a brief moment to the glass prisons we pass around the circle.

"Put them back, exactly where you found them," the naturalist instructs. "Turn the rocks back into place." "Leave the woods just as you found it." The sharing is the reward. There is no trophy to take home. All living things are returned to their safe place in the web of life.

Using activities from the "LEAF" curriculum, published by the Wisconsin Center for Environmental Education, the students learn to identify the trees by noticing differences in the bark and placement of the leaves and needles. "That big tree..." now has a name; it is an oak or a maple. We will respect it like a friend. We teach by slowing down, by stopping, in fact, to notice the small miracles alive in this forest. We Americans rush through our days. It is hard to teach "slowness." Students scout out living things, like insects, centipedes, newts, and salamanders that live under logs and rocks, and view them through hand-held lenses. The children delight in games that teach lessons in survival of species and the balance in nature. Continuous miracles unfold around a child who sits undisturbed and watches and listens. Careful drawings of a special tree are created, with words in a journal to accompany them. All these experiences add to an appreciation of the forest and the life that it sustains. As adults we can hope that the child who learns about the forest will grow to love, understand, and value it, and that the child will pass that knowledge and those values on to a generation we will never meet.

A forest curriculum is in its planning stages to assure that the high school students become good stewards of the forest, focusing on forest ecology, sustainable forestry management, and the economy of this community. Students could develop a business plan for the forest, perhaps developing advertising materials in computer graphic classes. They could make frames, furniture, bowls, or carvings to sell. They could study construction techniques. There is no better way to learn something than to have a "live" project, a living, working forest.

The Richter Forest changes with every season. But it is in spring, which arrives late here because of the cold water of the lake, when I notice the forest most. Tiny mayflowers stretch with blooms while the snow is still visible. Trilliums cover the forest floor with a living carpet of white and green as Memorial Day approaches.

Many birds, like the woodpecker, chickadee, white-breasted nuthatch, and northern cardinal, stay all year. In summer, the forest fills with birds. Red-eyed vireos, American redstarts, indigo buntings, wood thrush and rose-breasted grosbeak are commonly seen while walking in this forest.

Located on the southern-most tip of the island, the Richter Forest is a perfect place for migrant drops. When the weather conditions are right the migrant birds, moving on to their breeding grounds, often arrive here in great numbers. This is especially common in spring. Many species of warblers and other birds too rest here before they continue their journey to other places.

When the bright red and orange maples wave against the backdrop of the brilliant blue October sky, the cycle of the seasons is nearly complete. The surrounding water and its warmth allow autumn to linger just a little longer here than on the peninsula.

Soon the deciduous trees with dark, empty branches will stand guard with the green conifers in the snow-laden forest until the warmth of spring brings a new beginning to the cycle. Cross-country skiers and folks with snowshoes will enjoy this time to observe the animals and birds that find shelter and food in the forest.

In the Richter Forest a visitor can experience a sense of reverence for the land and for the people who walked here for generations. The forest offers us hope that as the world around us continues to change, this place will remain the same, thanks to the Richter gift, and offer those that follow after us a place of beauty, peace, and promise.

Through Winter Woods
by Bill Olson

Shush, shush, schushhhhhh
As skis slide over snow.
I hear no other sound
Until I stop,
And listen.
A distant dog barks.
Silence.
Silence.
A raucous jay.
Silence.
A flitting chick-a-dee-dee-dee.
Shush, shush.
No wind
To tease the trees,
Just a quiet white blanket
Disturbed only
By my skis and poles.
Down —
Shushhhhhh.
Up —
Shush, shush, shush, shush.
I head for home,
And winter woods
Regain their solitude.

A Place of Hope
(Bayshore Blufflands)

by Dan Burke

It was, I suppose, the most surreal experience I've ever had. While driving north from Sturgeon Bay along bucolic Bay Shore Drive I suddenly found myself yielding to a flock of free-range sheep. Although a newcomer to the peninsula, I never imagined I could be held up on a well-traveled Door County highway by a sheep blockade. But there I was, idling, watching as hundreds of aimless sheep crossed the road to graze contentedly on the groomed front lawns of dozens of lake shore properties. As curious as this scene was given the apparent absence of any nearby farm, an even more indelible and lasting impression was left on me that day. Out my car window a breathtaking landscape stretched out over the eastern horizon where a red blaze of sumac illuminated the top of a wind-swept field and majestic pines rose high above a sheer rock bluff that was aglow in autumn's finest hues. Now *this* is Door County, I remember thinking.

That unforgettable day was my first introduction to this serene landscape that I have come to know quite intimately. Although I have visited her countless times over the years, the Blufflands, as she is affectionately called, still never fails to fill me with hope and inspiration. She'll do the same for you, too, especially if you allow yourself the time to search out her many secret places and her spectacular panoramic vistas. But know this: a single visit will not do her justice, for every season brings her a fresh look worthy of more than just a casual gaze. Visit often, stay awhile — the Blufflands is sure to deliver every time.

Hugging the eastern shores of Green Bay, eight miles north of Sturgeon Bay, the Bayshore Blufflands is a grand landscape filled with scenery straight out of a picture postcard. But the Blufflands will surprise you with her subtlety as well. The rare ram's head lady's-slipper orchid with a flower no bigger than a fingernail was recently discovered here. So too were microscopic land snails that have survived in the cool, damp shade of the bluffs since the last period of glaciation. The dainty polypoddy fern defies all odds by eking out an existence on the talus slope of the escarpment. And tiny water flies dance and skip atop pools of crystal-clear spring water. Small wonders are as much a part of this place as are the towering rock walls, century-old red pines, and stretches of cobbled lakeshore as far as the eye can see.

The most significant feature of the Blufflands landscape is the rugged outcrop of the Niagara Escarpment that runs like a spine down the entire length of the preserve. The escarpment not only delivers some of the Midwest's most impressive scenic overlooks, but its unique soil and microclimate conditions offer a highly specialized habitat that is home for some species not found elsewhere in the county. The story of the escarpment begins some 450 million years ago when Wisconsin was a submerged equatorial landmass. It was then that the dolostones that make up today's escarpment were formed by the calcium-rich bodies of the coral, brachiopods, trilobites, cephalopods and snails that lived in warm, shallow seas. This ancient sea lay in a depression of the earth's crust, the center of which is now the state of Michigan. The outer edge of this ancient sea, lined with coral reefs, is what we now call the Niagara Escarpment. The escarpment runs from Niagara Falls in New York state through Ontario, Canada along the northern edges of lakes Ontario and Huron and then into the United States when it curves south into Wisconsin along the Door Peninsula.

Just as coral seas and walls of glacial ice formed this landscape over the ages, a cast of intriguing human characters has more recently played a hand in shaping the Blufflands. Among its ranks was an Illinois attorney who over a hundred years ago acquired nearly all of the lakeshore property here and commissioned a magnificent stone house to be built for his wife's summer getaway. This was before Bay Shore Drive existed, so when the couple finally made their way to their outpost, legend has it she took one look around and said "If you think I'm going to spend my days in this wilderness, you're crazy!"

But many people did choose to settle the area. Evidence from these earlier times is found at the base of the Niagara Escarpment where the historic Stage Road Trail can still be followed uninterrupted for miles. This trail was the main supply route that once connected Sturgeon Bay with Egg Harbor. Portions of the Stage Road Trail now serve as one of the many outstanding hiking trails at the Blufflands Preserve. Hiking paths are prevalent at the Blufflands thanks in large part to an eccentric resort owner who decades ago had grand plans of turning hundreds of acres here into one of the Midwest's finest tourist destinations.

The old Chateau Hutter Resort buildings are still a presence along the lakeshore south of Carlsville Road, and other imprints on the present-day landscape offer clues to the many dreams Mr. Hutter had for his property. A forest clearing is all that remains of a seldom-used ski hill he sculpted out of the escarpment. Another large clearing at the base of the bluff was home to a makeshift golf course where only a few hardcore links fans ever laid their cleats. A plane or two might have attempted a landing on the rough grassy surface of a runway he cut out. As for why there are so many hiking paths today, they originally served as horseback and recreational trails for resort guests.

Landowners, and the dreams they carry with them come and go through time, but one thing is always certain: Mother Nature, if left alone for any length of time, has a remarkable way of reclaiming what was once hers. This is certainly the case at the Blufflands. Forests cleared for timber, farms, and resorts now provide habitat for several rare grassland nesting birds including the northern goshawk, red-shouldered hawk, Cooper's hawk, veery, orchard oriole, grasshopper sparrow and eastern meadowlark. A half-mile road carved through a pristine woods to service a developer's planned, but never realized, subdivision is but a scar on this now-protected landscape. And as far as the flock of sheep that once roamed freely throughout the neighborhood, rumor has it they were rounded up and trucked away under the cover of darkness. I suppose area residents and officials never did quite warm up to their woolly, free-spirited neighbors.

At nearly 400 protected acres, the Blufflands has emerged as one of the Midwest's premier nature preserves. Pretty remarkable considering that not a single acre was under protection just a decade ago. Having served on the front lines of Door County's land conservation movement for many years, I know first-hand the hard work, money, and good fortune needed to preserve a single acre of land, not to mention an entire landscape. So what made the establishment of the Blufflands Preserve possible? How in 10 years did the Door County Land Trust manage to piece together hundreds of contiguous acres of field, forest, lakeshore, and bluff in the face of soaring land prices and escalating development pressures? Much of the credit goes to the "preserve makers," those, who through their countless giving of time, talent, and money, paved the way for the Blufflands establishment.

One of the most important of these preserve makers is Mary Standish, who along with her husband Michael own and have protected 16 acres of forest and lakeshore in the Blufflands. Mary didn't need any convincing that this was a place worth protecting, but even she must have been surprised by what she came upon during a routine walk in the woods in 1995. Mary was already aware that several rare plants called her neighborhood home including the Hooker's orchid, small yellow lady slipper, white-flowered ground cherry, longspur violet, and climbing fumitory. But discovering a colony of ram's-head lady's slipper, an exquisite orchid once thought to be confined to the Ridges Sanctuary and only a few other sites in the northern Great Lakes region, was most unexpected. Since the property where the orchids resided was for sale, she immediately contacted the local conservation organizations for assistance in protecting this rare find. The Land Trust responded and thus, with the purchase of a one-acre tract of land, the Bayshore Blufflands Preserve was born.

No story of the Blufflands is complete without acknowledging the work and vision of two people, Nancy Aten and Dan Collins. Together, they have purchased and permanently protected over 100 acres of springs, wetland, and forest. They perhaps best capture the spirit of the Blufflands in a letter they wrote regarding why, as a young couple, they decided to devote so much of their time and money to caring for land here. "I think of this land as borrowed," they write. "The opportunity to protect and restore 100 acres is more than we ever thought possible. The work of managing and removing the invasive plant species that are threatening the land's ecological health is of great satisfaction and pleasure to us; we can see the land responding. While we do this work, we are constantly enriched — seeing a heron rising from the pond, the first reddish sprouts of *pedicularis* in spring, the blooms of the wetland sedges, a salamander, a snake, the vibrant fruit of *viburnum trilobum* in the fall. We are borrowing this place, hopefully with enough time for us to make significant restoration progress, so that when we're gone, it can be given back entirely to the wild."

The Blufflands has and continues to mean different things to different people. To me, she represents hope at a time when critical wildlife habitat and scenic open space is being lost at an unprecedented rate. If we can save the Blufflands can't we too preserve the other special places in Door County that are deserving of protection? Land preservation success stories are more important now than ever before and the Blufflands will forever serve as a model for how passionate people can make a lasting difference.

Three Wishes
by Estella Lauter

Last spring, we walked below the bluff
at the end of the Door Peninsula
to see the rock art made by Indian
Anishinaabe fishermen
more than a century ago: an elk
a thunderbird and two canoes.

Signs on a map for hunters far
from home, they also served as spirit guides.
Come here, the artists said, *where
your ancestors found food and power.*

Even faded by sun, wind
and time, these paintings made from tough
red roots and sturgeon oil
remain on this protected cliff.

In this art we find three wishes:
duration—a long life filled
with rich encounters together;
creativity—the will
to make the most of what you see;
commitment—not just to yourselves but to
the ones who come after.

Touch the earth lightly, but leave
your marks so loving eyes can find them.

Kangaroo Lake As I See It

by Nancy Rafal

There is something special about the first steps one takes on new terrain, be it an exotic, faraway land or a nearby, open-to-the-public woodland. The impulse is to take this first time experience and knit it into personal history. In seeking to tame the event by searching for similarities to the known, one can, perhaps, feel more at home in an alien environment. Maybe it's a need to feel in control, or maybe a respect for the unknown, but a person seldom simply opens up and surrenders to the enjoyment of exploring the new. It could be that the curious child has been locked away in the overly cautious adult.

When I first encountered Kangaroo Lake some dozen years ago, I opted to let the experience wash over me and to relish in the discoveries I found there. Leaving my car in what is now The Nature Conservancy (TNC) parking area on the west side of the lake, I entered the woods one warm midday and began my descent toward the lake. Out of the beat of the sun I was enrobed in a silky coolness of the leaf canopy and was intoxicated by the rich earthy fragrance of regeneration. Each step took me further into unknown territory and out of the straitjacket of my life in a Chicago suburb. Tensions eased and fell away to forest duff. My steps became bouncy, muscles relaxed. My breathing deepened, reaching into the pit of my lungs, where fresh clean air began replacing the polluted city vapors. On that first walk I gave myself over to nature and came away sated, completed, fulfilled, renewed.

Kangaroo Lake has two faces like the god Janus in Greek mythology. The north end is shallower and is surrounded by mud flats and sedge mats. The larger southern lobe has vacation homes accompanied by summer motorboats and winter snowmobiles. The northern waters are free of such intrusions except for a few cottages west of the causeway. In the late 1800s the County Highway E causeway was built, emphasizing the Janus quality: under the causeway a trio of culverts allows water to flow north to south.

Kangaroo Lake is a shallow marl bottom lake of 1,122 acres. Marl

lakes are not common but Door County has many due to past and
continuing calcium carbonate precipitation from dolomite stone into
lake basins. On geological maps it is clear that Kangaroo Lake lies in a
shallow trough of the Niagara Escarpment. Peil Creek flows into the
lake from the north and Hines Creek begins at the southeast corner of
the lake and terminates at Lake Michigan.

There is geologic evidence that the lake was created by postglacial
rebound as Lake Algonquin, 8000 BP (years before present), and Lake
Nipissing, 4000 BP, receded and sand was deposited, making an
embayment. The dolomite plateau west of the lake rises 110 feet above
the lake surface and is exposed in places. The area has a high concentration of bedrock crevices and fracture traces. This plateau is most
likely where rainwater begins a journey to the numerous springs
along Peil Creek. Some of these springs can be observed where the
creek enters the lake.

I recognized when I first walked the plateau that the north Kangaroo Lake area was special. Personally I felt closer to something basic
and I felt a connection to the natural landscape. I knew that development could bring vacation homes, condominiums, motor boats, and
jet skis, and would degrade habitat for water fowl, songbirds, and
wildflowers. I'd seen it happen in DuPage County, west of Chicago,
where whole sections of land were stripped of top soil and tracts of
houses, strip malls, and pavement expanded at an ever-increasing
rate, gobbling up farm and woodlands. DuPage County has become
the center of an urban sprawl that now eats its way west through
neighboring Kane County and beyond. A sense of sadness came over
me as I anticipated this dismal fate for Kangaroo Lake.

A surprise awaited me on my initial foray. I continued to descend
the unmarked path knowing I would come to the lake eventually. The
path angled south along an elevated ridge, possibly an ancient ice
shove. Walking along the shore I found a tree stump that had been
carved into a primitive face. It looks east over the water and, to me at
least, is a symbol of protection of this environmentally significant
area. I don't know who carved the figure or when it was done, but I
know I feel a connection every time I reach this spot on my hike. It is
important for me to touch the stump in thanks to all the people and
groups that have ventured to preserve the natural habitat here and
throughout our world.

The face reminds me of the Iroquois' wisdom of considering the
impact on their great-, great-, great-, great-, great-grandchildren, the
seventh generation, in all decision making. It would be wise of us to
consider how our land use decisions will impact the earth seven generations hence.

During my years in Door County I've learned about some significant land preservation efforts. Fortunately both TNC and the Door County Land Trust (DCLT) have been active in the Kangaroo Lake area. In 1995, TNC and the DCLT announced the formation of the Kangaroo Lake Ecopreserve as a tool to preserve the natural landscape of the north end of the lake and of Peil Creek, which feeds into it. Roughly 2,500 acres are within the ecopreserve boundaries. Not all are owned by TNC and the DCLT. Some landowners have entered conservation easement agreements with the DCLT or are using other means to halt shoreline development.

TNC and the DCLT have been aided by a unique local group and by Wisconsin Department of Natural Resources (WisDNR). In 2002, the WisDNR designated a 357-acre area on Kangaroo Lake's north end as a State Natural Area. TNC and the DCLT own and manage the land but the designation is additional insurance for permanent protected status. The state's Natural Areas Program is the first of its kind in the country, and over 147,00 acres of environmentally sensitive Wisconsin land was protected by 2002. The acres continue to increase. Most State Natural Areas are open to the public for hiking and other low-impact recreational activities. The Kangaroo Lake facility is open from dawn to dusk, year round.

Another means of protection is the Wisconsin Knowles-Nelson Stewardship Program. This program was established in 1989 to expand opportunities for outdoor recreation, restore wildlife habit, preserve natural areas and protect water quality. The program is administered through the WisDNR and provides 50 percent matching grants to local governments and nonprofit organizations. In 2001 TNC received a Knowles-Nelson Stewardship Grant of $203,750 toward the Kangaroo Lake project.

Each of these organizations is made up of individuals who are dedicated to keeping nature in our lives and keeping nature working for the earth. They are part of the circle of connectivity. Through the work of these good people we can experience the wonders of first steps on new terrain and the many more wonders of preserved natural spaces such as the north end of Kangaroo Lake.

On my initial west side walk I was ignorant of the plant and animal names but I felt akin to their rhythms and sister to their cycles. On a recent venture in early fall some of joy of discovery came back to me. Punctuating my walk were blue berries on leafless stalks. This time I knew the name of the plant: blue cohash.

My mentors in learning plant names have been Roy and Charlotte Lukes. The Lukes are well-respected naturalists. He was director of the Ridges Sanctuary in Baileys Harbor for close to 30 years. She has become an expert on area mushrooms. Roy and Charlotte were introduced by Eunice Caron in 1971. Charlotte was Louis and Eunice Caron's dental hygienist in Milwaukee. The Carons owned a house and property on Maple Road northwest of Kangaroo Lake. The parcel is currently owned by Karl and Lucy Klug who have entered a conservation easement agreement with the DCLT. The circle of connectivity just keeps growing

I have spent a sunny May afternoon with Lucy Klug walking the trails through their property. In the spring wildflowers abound in the woods of this preserved 40 acres. The Klugs have documented hepatica, spring beauty, Dutchman's breeches, squirrel corn, trout lily, wood anemone, wild leek, jack-in-the-pulpit, Indian pipe, shinleaf, beech drops, fringed polygala, sweet cicely, blue cohosh, Canada mayflower, yellow lady's slipper, ladies' tresses orchid, Solomon's plume, trillium, and several other wildflowers in the upland forest area around their home.

In the wetlands they have seen meadow equisetum, hairy skullcap, rush aster, purple aster, yarrow, fringed gentian, grass-of-Parnassus, yellow lady's slipper, joe-pye weed, boneset, marsh bellflower, Kalm's lobelia, turtlehead, prairie loosestrife, and silverweed.

In the meadow lands there are pussy toes, Queen Anne's lace, oxeye daisy, blue flax, blue-eyed grass, St. John's wort, hawkweed, black-eyed Susan, thimbleweed, goldenrods, New England aster, crooked stem aster, bergamot, heather aster, and coreopsis all blooming in their own time.

Like our forefathers, the Klugs seem to mark the passage of the seasons by what is in bloom or setting fruit.

The Klugs' woodland is typical of the north Kangaroo Lake foliage. Sprinkled with sugar maple, American beech, white birch, and red oak, it is a glorious sight in all seasons. Canada yew, star flowers, goldthread, and naked miterwort dot the forest floor. Blue cohosh blossoms give way to startling blue berries in the fall.

Wildlife abounds at Kangaroo Lake. The lake provides seasonal feeding and resting areas for migrating waterfowl. Canada geese feed on bulrushes in the fall, and puddle and diving ducks feed in the basin during migration; shorebirds use both mud flats and sedge mats. The list is long: American black duck, mallard, northern pintail, wood duck, ring-necked duck, blue-winged teal, hooded merganser, shoveler, greater scaup, lesser scaup, bufflehead, common goldeneye, green-winged teal.

The haunting call of the sandhill crane is heard throughout the summer and kingfishers bedeck utility poles along the causeway. While bald eagles, osprey, and Caspian terns nest along nearby Lake

Michigan shores they fly the short distance west to feed in the calmer, shallow waters of Kangaroo Lake. In addition to the usual range of Wisconsin warm-water fish, bowfin and gar have been found here. It appears that spawning areas are primarily located in the north 300-acre lobe of the lake. Throughout the summer adults and children fish from the causeway, and in the winter ice shanties can be seen.

In the spring of 2005 TNC purchased 42 acres located on Peil Creek. It is a critical wetland parcel at the headwaters of Kangaroo Lake. A generous gift of $250,000 was made to TNC in memory of Judy Abert Meissner. David Meissner introduced his bride to Door County and the couple spent many happy times in Door County with family and friends. Judy died of ovarian cancer in 2003. Judy's husband, along with her brother and sister, are responsible for the gift, and the parcel is now identified by a sign: Judy Abert Meissner Memorial Wetlands Preserve.

In the fall of 2005 I made my first visit to the Meissner Preserve. An unmarked path leads from a miniscule parking lot along an orchard and down to wetlands. I felt that same thrill of discovery I'd felt years ago at Kangaroo Lake. I've become good at clearing my mind and calling up childlike curiosities. While I didn't find a face carved in a stump I did find evidence of land stewardship. Ten acres of the preserve is being planted with white pine, white spruce, red oak, ash, and aspen trees. This parcel has good potential as a breeding habitat for the federally protected Hine's emerald dragonfly. It is also the only site in Wisconsin for a rare land snail.

It takes many individuals and organizations to preserve land. Municipalities need officials who see value in land left to nature's whims. Vacant recreational land does not bring in the tax revenue of buildings and parking lots. However, studies have been done that show that undeveloped lands don't cost as much as developed lands when it comes to requiring municipal services and infrastructure.

We all need time with nature to recharge our batteries and to be connected with the earth. I look forward to the day when I can walk to that lakeside face-in-the-stump and know that most of the land within the Kangaroo Lake Ecopreserve is actually under protection and that we can pass this legacy down to the seventh generation.

Robert LaSalle County Park:
Southern Door County's Sunrise Surprise
(Southern Shores)
by George K. Pinney

In 1927, the Door County Board of Supervisors formed a park committee and instructed them to purchase land near the historic village of Williamsville (Tornado Park) and in the Mink River area. This was the beginning of the Door County Parks System, which today consists of 18 unique and varied parcels of land.

In 1929, approximately six acres of land was purchased on the shores of Lake Michigan in the Town of Union, near the southern end of Door County. This site is believed to have been a landing point of the French explorer Robert L. LaSalle in 1679. Thus, the park was named Robert LaSalle County Park. In 1942, an additional two acres was donated on the south edge of the park to include a large ravine where a small creek cuts through the sand beach terraces to Lake Michigan. In 1956, a small parcel to the north was purchased for additional parking. Finally, in 2004, a half-mile long, 16-acre parcel was purchased on the north side of the park.

Robert LaSalle Park, located on County Trunk U near the southern end of Door County, on the shores of Lake Michigan, consists of three levels of land. The first level is on the shores of Lake Michigan where a sand and stone beach provides water access. The upper two levels of the park are ancient shorelines of Lake Michigan. The second level, called Lower LaSalle, is accessed from Lower LaSalle Road. This level is approximately 10 feet above the waters of the lake. The south end of the park is part of the original purchase and consists of an open grass area with picnic tables, grills, and parking. The ravine is easily accessed from this level on the south, as is the half-mile long pine plantation on the north. The third level, called Upper LaSalle, is accessed from County Trunk U and is 100 feet above the waters of Lake Michigan. The south end of this level is also a part of the original purchase and affords an outstanding view of the creek from the top of the 60-foot ravine. Restrooms, picnic tables, grills, and parking are located in this area. The north end of this level is a part of the 2004 purchase that was a farm field and provides an "above the treetops" view of Lake Michigan. The 2004 addition will be developed with trails and viewing areas in the future. Stairs located within the original purchase connect the three levels of the park.

Many people have written about LaSalle Park and the history of the area, but one of the most informative articles was written by H.R. Holland in 1930, shortly after the park was purchased. Mr. Holland was a member of the park board in the '30s and '40s and was instrumental in the purchase of many of the parks we enjoy today. My father, Thomas S. Pinney, Sr., was secretary of the parks board in the 1940s and worked with Mr. Holland in acquiring and developing our county park system. H.R. Holland wrote in the *Peninsula Historical Review*, Vol. IV. June, 1930 the following:

"With the excellent help of the Door County Parks Commission the Door County Historical Society has now secured the preservation of another most interesting historic spot in Door County. This will hereafter be known as the Robert LaSalle County Park. This name is given to it because Robert LaSalle, the greatest of the American explorers, on his expedition to explore the Mississippi valley in 1679, met with a most interesting adventure at this place. The park lies about ten miles south of Sturgeon Bay on the Lake Michigan shore, and embraces about six acres of land, which lies between County Trunk U and Lake Michigan.

"County Trunk U is one of the most picturesque highways in Door County. Starting out at Sawyer, it meanders over hill and dale with numerous charming curves under arching trees. Every mile or so a glimpse of the great lake is visible over rolling fields of green. Nine miles south of the city the highway leaves the highlands and follows the beach past the old historic village of Clay Banks—once the largest shipping point for forest products on the peninsula, but now a collection of tottering ruins. To this place hundreds of early homesteaders back in the woods with their oxen daily hauled their telegraph poles, ties and timber of all kinds, fearfully pondering what the future would have in store for them when this source of income would come to an end, for farming was then considered a doubtful problem so far north. But now the timber and the stumps are all gone and Clay Banks—the township that lies back of the former village—is one of the best developed and most productive farming sections in Wisconsin.

"Just south of the old village, the highway climbs up a long hill, from the top of which one has the finest view of Lake Michigan along its entire western shore. This is also the highest point on the shore north of Chicago. At this place the land rises almost 200 feet above the water by means of a precipitous bank of clay. This clay bank is an ancient landmark of the lake and was a guide for sailors more than a hundred years ago, long before the first lighthouse was built.

"From this noble elevation may be seen the finest vision of sunrise in all America west of the Atlantic coast. No smoke here hovers to blur the delicate tints of Nature; no noise to disturb the serene sublimity of the surroundings. In the early dawn the shimmering surface of the lake appears with a clearer color of gray than the cloud-flecked vault of the sky above. Then far in the east, those dark clouds imperceptibly change to feathery mists of milky foam with edges of glowing pink. Soon the entire horizon is a wonderland of color, until finally the sun appears, changing the lake below to a sheen of silver and the floating clouds to castles of gold.

"Just a quarter mile south of this imposing headland lies Robert LaSalle Park. Here is one of the most scenic spots along the Lake Michigan shore, for, through some fortunate accidents, several adjoining timber groves have here been spared to add their charm to other lakeside delights. Although the park includes only six acres of land, it has several distinct configurations of scenic beauty. The upper part of the park which is first seen from the highway is a level terrace having an elevation of about a hundred feet above the lake. A well wooded hillside which bisects the park leads down to a lower plain of two or three acres laying along the shore, making a most charming place for campers or for outdoors sports. On the southern edge of the park runs a deep ravine from the highway to the lake. This picturesque ravine has great possibilities of beauty, but, unfortunately, only the upper part lies within the area of the park. The boundary line bisects it obliquely in the most unsatisfactory manner. It is to be hoped that the entire ravine will eventually be included in the park.

"Upon the recommendation of the Door County Historical Society, the County Park Commission asked the County Board for one thousand dollars to buy and improve the lands within the proposed park. This was generously and unanimously granted. Upon solicitation the Town of Clay Banks also appropriated three hundred dollars which was immediately place in the hands of the Historical Society. A number of farmers of Clay Banks also left their plowing and seeding one day and spent their time in pulling stumps, burning brush, plowing, etc., and accomplished a vast amount of labor. At that time 1700 evergreens were planted in the park under the supervision of some members of the Historical Society.

The $1,300.00 available for the park proved amply sufficient. The land cost $734.00. Almost two hundred dollars has been used for blasting stumps, plowing, scraping, seeding and planting. This spring an imposed gateway and fence of cedar work has been constructed at a cost of about three hundred dollars. We think this gateway and fence is the most artistic thing of its kind in the county, but perhaps it is best to wait for the verdict of *vox populi*. The gateposts at least are unique. We wanted two logs upwards of three feet in diameter, and as the schooners of old Clay Banks long since carried away the last of such dimensions from this vicinity, it was necessary to send to the Pacific Coast for them. A row of elms has been planted along the highway in front of the park.

"As usual the business men of Sturgeon Bay have generously given their assistance when asked. This time it was necessary to ask only two. Mr. Brower of the Leathem Smith Co. generously gave us the benefit of the wholesale price on the lings from Washington and moreover paid the freight and drayage charges right to the park. Mr. Peterson, manager of the Van Camp Condensery, also kindly sent two of his largest trucks twenty miles north into the county and hauled down the three hundred posts and poles needed for the fence free of charge.

"It now remains to erect a suitable monument in honor of Robert LaSalle for whom the park is named. A pillar of weathered limestone, ideal for the purpose, has been found. It is about eight feet high and will be erected on a small knoll. A bronze tablet will be affixed to it, bearing an inscription which will tell briefly the reason for the creation of the park. At a recent meeting of the Board of Directors of the Historical Society, the board appropriated $375.00 to pay for this marker and to provide for suitable entertainment the time of the dedication of the park, which is planned for some day next August."
                                        —H.R. Holland

Today the park is quite similar to Mr. Holland's report in many ways. A small pavilion has come and gone, as has a drinking water well since his report. The cedar fence no longer remains. But the gate posts made of three foot diameter logs from Washington State still remain, as does the serenity of the view and morning sunrises. County Trunk U, in the area of LaSalle Park, is still the picturesque road that Mr. Holland describes and remains a lightly traveled route. Sunrise over Lake Michigan viewed from the park remain the same, breathtaking and awe inspiring.

Reactions to Extinction
by Loraine Brink

*After learning that the Hine's emerald dragonfly faces extinction
due to the destruction of its habitat, winged envoys of the insect
world convened to discuss their plight.*
—Swamp Headquarters Bulletin

The darning-needle dragonflies objected to the fray.
*We dart about on delicate wings, translucent in the sun.
Our slender needles pierce the air more graceful than the one
they call Hine's. We feel no urgency about these signs.*

The gypsy moths laughed raucously. *The irony is this,
they're spending more to keep the Hine's
than to expurgate, eliminate, eradicate our kind.*

The shapely luna moths in fluid green expressed dismay.
*Admirers love our Renoir flair. Unthinkable to share
with Emerald.*

The bumbles, wasps, and honeybees were totally provoked
*No time for dragonflies right now. We sting,
we buzz the folks outdoors. This season is our fun.*

Remaining calm and self-composed, the monarchs stayed serene.
*Our friends last week located a marsh where emerald can survive.
A site on Kangaroo Lake, few humans, fewer cars, a place
we all aspire to—an insect Shangri-La.*

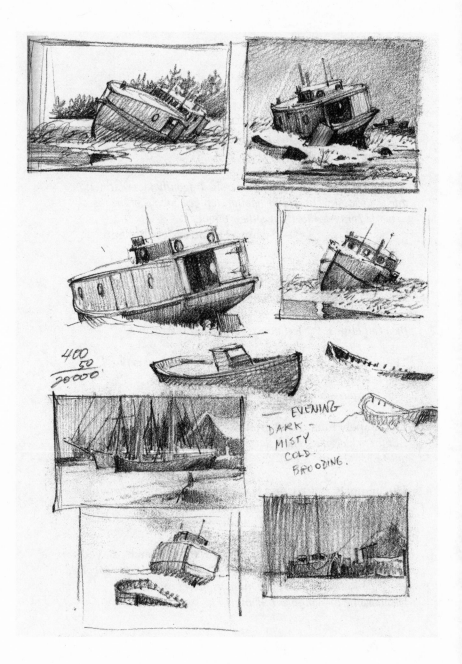

400
50
20000

EVENING
DARK -
MISTY
COLD.
BROODING.

Detroit Harbor Preserve, Washington Island
By Dick Purinton

The State of Wisconsin declared Detroit Harbor a State Natural Area because of its uniqueness and importance.

Rare or endangered plant and animal species are found there. The critical habitat of Detroit Harbor, "the intermittent, emergent wetlands" as described by professional naturalists, supports a variety of plant and animal species, including several listed as rare or endangered, such as the dwarf lake iris, Crawe's sedge, low calamint, and the Hine's emerald dragonfly. In addition, dozens of other plant, insect, bird, animal, and fish species have been observed in the four seasons. The harbor is also home to nesting and transient water birds: great blue herons, kingfishers, geese, swans, and many varieties of ducks. Eagles have successfully nested on Detroit Island, and they have been spotted soaring over the harbor looking for prey.

A State Natural Area designation is significant. It may also seem a bit surprising to discover such diversity within a harbor that receives thousands of visitors each year. The daily, year-round movement of ferry traffic is centered at the island terminal in the West Channel of Detroit Harbor and qualifies this as the busiest of all Door County harbors. Nearly 4,000 annual ferry arrivals support a tourism economy, bringing people, cars, trucks, trailers, and freight to Washington Island. In addition, on a given summer's day a variety of recreational boating may be seen: kayaks, jet skis, rowboats, motorized fishing boats, sailboats, and cruising yachts from all over the Great Lakes, which find safe anchorage for the night. In the fall, duck hunters hunker behind blinds or paddle the shores in duck boats, and in November deer hunters stalk the shoreline woods and roughs. As soon as harbor ice is thick enough, fishermen and their shanties dot the harbor, setting tip-ups and jigging for perch and northern pike.

The human activity and development that often accompany people have so far spared many of the critical sections of Detroit Harbor. Ferry and marina activity is concentrated in two main locations, near the East and West Channels. Other than these sites, public access to the harbor is very limited. There is a town launching ramp at Lobdell's Point and a small beach park near the Red Barn, adjacent to the Shipyard Marina. A glimpse of the harbor can also be seen from the end of Main Road. Otherwise, access to the harbor is by water-craft, or by private property.

Pleasure boating and ferry activity are most intense over a three-month period in summer, tapering to nearly zero by the time ice has set in. Winter and a cold, prolonged spring also reduce human presence, giving the land a chance to rest, but also discouraging expansion of tourism to a viable year-round industry.

Because the harbor's appeal is so seasonal and visits to island properties must be coordinated with ferry schedules, property values per acre or per front foot along the shore are lower than on the mainland. Business investment carries with it lower volume and higher risk of failure than a similar business on the Door Peninsula. In addition, past trends of very measured growth and attractive real estate prices don't stay constant. Interest in shore properties leads to land development that begins to chip away at the harbor margins, even though the pace is slower than in harbors on the Peninsula.

A proactive effort to identify and preserve key properties for their natural value within the harbor has begun, so that when development occurs, it won't be in areas critical to habitat. These conservancy lands are managed with conservation easements and agreed upon goals, co-ordinated between several nonprofit organizations, the Door County Land Trust and the Nature Conservancy, the State of Wisconsin, and private landowners.

The geography: What is Detroit Harbor like?

Detroit Harbor is Washington Island's southernmost harbor. It is nearest in proximity to the Door Peninsula's northern tip and connecting highways, approximately three miles from the Northport ferry dock as the eagle flies.

Irregularly shaped, it has many inlets, twists, and turns along its shoreline. Islands and reefs, channels and sloughs, sandbars and rock piles, reedy shallows, and an estuary called the Bayou describe the variety found there. Two channel entrances promote nearly continual flow of currents, and yet the harbor is well protected from all compass points from the direct seas of Lake Michigan. The inner portion of Detroit Harbor ranges from a few inches to 10 feet at its deepest, and this moderate depth makes it accessible to shallower-draft watercraft, but prevents much larger, deeper-draft vessels from entering.

The present-day vehicle and passenger ferries draw up to 10 feet and must confine maneuvering to the West Channel, dredged by the Army Corps of Engineers to 17 feet in the 1930s. At the opposite side of the harbor is the East Channel, guarded by rock piles and shallows. Only skilled bass fishermen and old-timers who know visual ranges attempt to navigate the East Channel where the bottom can vary from rocky reefs to sandy flats.

The two channels act like a pair of open windows on opposite sides of a home in hot weather: water flows in one side and out the other. Winds drive the water, building up pressure within the harbor, and flood the shallows and the estuary. Water then flows out the opposite channel. Passengers on ferries sometimes ask about the current line where milky harbor water mixes with blue, cooler lake waters near Plum Island. Current can flow from this channel at several miles per hour, and it does even in winter when pieces of ice broken by ferry propellers sweep past the pier ends.

Nature's flushing action refreshes Detroit Harbor's waters, and in addition springs are found in the shallows near the end of Main Road, and there is drainage from upland cedar swamps, all of which contribute to the water's quality and characteristics. This integration of water sources, plus highly alkaline water from the limestone soils, tempered and warmed within the inlets and bays, are underlying reasons why unique and diverse plant and animal habitat is found there. One result of such a confluence is the excellent small mouth bass spawning grounds found in Detroit Harbor, one of the finest in northern Lake Michigan according to state fisheries experts.

Dead Horse Island and Richter's Point are two seemingly insignificant harbor features typically found in the harbor. These features play an important role by turning the harbor currents and funneling water between them.

Cedars, popple, and alders grow along the banks and in adjacent wetlands. Varieties of northern hardwoods and conifers are found at slightly higher elevation where soils are drained. Along these harbor margins are found larger mammals such as white-tail deer, muskrat, an occasional beaver, red and gray fox, and raccoons, along with a variety of birds mentioned earlier, including songbirds. Many of these species can be easily observed by anyone who takes the time. On many occasions passengers will spot the larger, more obvious birds such as eagles, swans, geese, pelicans, gulls, and terns — and cormorants.

Detroit Harbor: The human factor

Native Americans encamped along Detroit Harbor's shores well over 2,000 years before Europeans arrived. An archeological team from the University of Wisconsin-Milwaukee in 1968 uncovered artifacts and human remains in a sandy pasture at the end of Main Road. Carbon dating determined the site to have been occupied at 200 A.D.

Natives were here when French voyageurs — who were fur traders, explorers and missionaries — arrived in the 1600s by canoe. Nicolet, Raddison, and Marquette were among those who paddled the chain of islands they named the Grand Traverse Islands, islands scattered like stepping stones northward from the Door passage to Michigan's Upper Peninsula. More than likely the voyageurs had also paddled their canoes into Detroit Harbor, which was paired with the nearby island that forms the harbor's southern coastline: Le Petit Detroit, meaning Little Detroit or little strait, a contrast with the other 'big' Detroit between Lake Huron and Lake Erie. A small band of Ottawas lived on Little Detroit during French visits in late 1700s through the early 1800s.
                    —Conan Eaton, The Naming, 1966

LaSalle's arrival in the Great Lakes' first sailing ship, Griffin, in 1679 gained the greatest notoriety of all French explorers to this area, partly due to the detailed journals of Father Hennepin, a Jesuit who accompanied LaSalle, and also to the mystery of the Griffin's loss. The Griffin, with its load of furs, disappeared soon after departing these islands for eastern Lake Erie.

(According to the *Door County Advocate*'s nautical affairs column by Jon Paul, November 26-27, 2005, an underwater research group claims to have found the wreck of the Griffin north of St. Martin's Island. This is not the first such claim, but it has drawn great interest, including that of the French government. LaSalle's Griffin was under royal charter, and therefore the French government has claimed her even after all these years, if the wreck can be identified as such. The matter will be argued in Federal Court.)

British occupation followed the French and Indian Wars, and they further exploited the upper Midwest fur trade late into the late 1700s. Britain did not cede control of the upper Great Lakes to the United States until several years after the War of 1812. Little written history survives from this period or prior years, but we know from artifacts that the Grand Traverse Islands, and in particular Rock, Washington, and Detroit Islands were a meeting place between natives and fur traders. They were also a logical departure point as traders left Green

Bay waters for the Straits of Mackinac. One exception is the record of Father Baraga, a Roman Catholic priest who served numerous missions in lower Michigan and who devoted his later years to mission work in the Upper Peninsula of Michigan. Baraga in 1833 canoed 60 miles across open waters of Lake Michigan from Beaver Island — a feat we would not consider attempting today — to reestablish ties with natives at a mission on Detroit Island.

One year later, in 1834, two young men set up a fishing camp on Detroit Island and built a small cabin there, considered by Jesse Miner to be the first dwelling in Door County (discounting any previous huts or shelters built by French fur traders). The two men stayed there for over a year, until the men and their cabin came under attack by Indians. One man was killed; the other fled on a sailing ship passing through Death's Door Passage. Early Washington Island mail carrier, town official, and historian Jesse Miner made it seem as easy as hailing a cab on a busy Chicago street.

     —Jesse Miner, History and Anecdotes of Washington Island; from Island Tales, *prepared by Kay Curtis, c.1965*

This thwarted effort to establish roots on Detroit Island marked the first in successive settlement efforts by Europeans on the Grand Traverse Islands. Within two years of this incident, fishing families, not just single men, lived on Rock Island year-round, near a government lighthouse built there in 1836 for commercial shipping.

By the time the Civil War ended, Washington Island had become a major settlement in northeastern Wisconsin. Sailing schooners brought trade to its three main harbors: Jackson Harbor, Washington Harbor, and Detroit Harbor. Washington Island became a fueling stop when steam power took over from wind.

By 1900, a few sailing schooners entered Detroit Harbor with centerboards raised. But most trade was by smaller, motorized vessels called hookers that traded goods and carried passengers to Green Bay, Escanaba, and the Door Peninsula. Once roads on the Door Peninsula became the established and preferred route to the county seat in Sturgeon Bay, about 1920, car ferries with scheduled service made their appearance.

Detroit Harbor's close proximity to the mainland became an advantage, and soon it eclipsed other island harbors with both ferry and small freighter trade. Sufficient natural depth at several harbor locations led to the construction of piers that fostered commerce, which in turn supported more development ashore.

An example of this was the Detroit Harbor Community near the

south end of Main Road, where the Ida Bo Inn, the Detroit Harbor
Post Office, and a store were located. Today a pile of old crib timbers
and rocks projects above water, just barely visible in front of the Holi-
day Inn. Less than a third of a mile east of that dock another pier was
the enterprise of Nor Shellswick, a Danish immigrant who built and
ran a boarding house and post office there.

Down the shoreline a bit farther, not far from the East Channel,
the Jensenville community sprang up. The center of early wooden
ferry activity in the 1920s was at the shipyard dock where there was
also a marine railway for hauling and repairing boats. The Washington Hotel invited guests for meals and rooms just up the road from
the ferry landing, and the Gislason family ran a general store to service customers in the little community. Cottages sprang up among
cedars along the rocky shoreline, as families from as far as St. Louis,
Chicago, and Pittsburgh were attracted to the island summer climate.

The ferry dock near Lobdell's Point, landing point for the Washington Island Ferry Line, became active only after 1930 when Capt.
Bill Jepson shortened his route to the mainland by shifting his land-
ings from the shipyard near the East Channel to the West Channel.
Adjacent to Jepson's landing was the Standard Oil dock (now
Hansen's dock), where oil products were offloaded. Commercial fish
tugs moored at what later became the Island Outpost (Cornell) and Island Clipper (Chambers) docks. Commercial fishermen also had
docks across the West Channel, on the inside arm of Detroit Island,
where depths were 10 feet right against shore. Several fishing families
lived there, Fred and Ida Richter among them. Richter's Point was
named for them.

Frequent and intimate navigation of the harbor by fishermen,
ferry crews, and other sailors led to names for harbor features too
small or insignificant to be found on official nautical charts. Such
place names, in addition to Richter's Point, are: Rabbit Point (the other
"ear" on Detroit Island), the Bayou (estuary), Kalmbach's swamp,
Susie's Island (named for Susan, a daughter of Gottfried and Christina
Kalmbach), Horseshoe Island, Pedersen's Bay, and Dead Horse Island
(where Capt. Pedersen's team of horses floated ashore in spring after
breaking through the harbor ice one winter).

Detroit Harbor's communities sprang up, and then faded with the
times. The economy shifted from fishing to logging to farming, with a
bit of tourism. By the end of the 1960s, it was primarily tourism that
supported the local economy, as the island's permanent population
dipped below 600. The island cheese factory closed; dairy farmers had
no local outlet for milk. The large potato farms of Ed Anderson went
out of business (Anderson also had notable efforts in developing land

on Detroit Island, building docks, and surveying and building roads there). When the economy closed in on the island, tourism seemed the only option left, the one that could still produce income for island business owners. Washington Island's Detroit Harbor was still a great place to visit by ferry, a pleasant boating destination for picnics or casting a lure.

Nature persists

Fortunately, since the establishment of Washington Township in June 1850 on Rock Island, man's footprint in Detroit Harbor had not been as heavy as perhaps it might have been. Protection of natural elements was achieved, to a great extent, through geographic isolation. Distance from the mainland and population centers, coupled with at least four months of ice and snow each year, equated to minimal ferry service in winter. But even in summer, the flow of visitors depended upon calm waters and ferries, and the urges of a certain type of visitor with curiosity about seeing what lies beyond the mainland.

The island's tourism economy during the last 50 years has been the major influence on the real estate market as buyers seek prime property for seasonal homes, especially along the shoreline. Land sales and development that followed resulted in the construction or remodeling of seasonal and year-round homes, which in turn supports numerous families with construction or service-related jobs.

The enjoyment of nature and a fondness for keeping things "as they are" has often been expressed as a key reason why people buy island property and choose to live, retire, or work on Washington Island. This desire to preserve a natural setting, along with island economics and location, are strong reasons why there hasn't been more aggressive development along Detroit Harbor's shores.

While we think of most newer homes in Detroit Harbor as being located on Washington Island, a number of summer homes have been built on Detroit Island, too. There, land values are slightly lower than for similar properties on Washington Island, and basic services are fewer. Detroit Island's property owners must be resourceful in providing their own services, services readily available to Washington Island's residents such as electricity, phone, solid waste disposal, fire protection, and emergency rescue. In addition, to get from Washington Island to their Detroit Island homes, property owners must motor across the channel from the ferry dock in private boats with their suitcases, groceries and provisions.

What about Detroit Harbor's future?

Conservancy areas contribute positively to landowners by sparing shoreline development in Detroit Harbor — an oxymoron of sorts. Leaving land in a natural state has been shown to lessen taxpayer burden for infrastructure, as compared with developed property. The undeveloped natural areas offer beauty, wildlife, and plant diversity that contribute to sport fishing, water sports, birding, photography, and the dozens of active and passive things people do when on vacation — or when they select a place to retire.

Human occupation on Washington and Detroit Islands and the economy to support a community will require ongoing development, but it is a matter of choosing wisely where to build and where to conserve. Without specifically dedicated natural areas, it becomes a matter of time — years, maybe decades — before more properties essential to the natural area are logged, bisected with roads and power lines, dug up with wastewater systems, and developed into building sites. Even when one development of a single property may seem incremental, the accumulative effect can disrupt soil absorption rates, change soil and air temperatures by increasing sunlight penetration, displace bird and animal life, and destroy plant and wildlife habitat. Once harmed, damage to the habitat is difficult, if not impossible, to reverse.

Appreciation for Detroit Harbor's conservancy areas, especially when expressed by island residents and property owners, is a sign of support for habitat succession into the next century and beyond.

The Last Boat
by Trygvie Jensen

Morning breaks with her devout silence
Over the harbor like amber glass.
Yesterday's storm and white-capped waves relent,
Leaving the harbor's hull a placid mass.

A weathered dock moors no boats
And slips down more to water's side;
A seasoned reflection still floats
Where once fish tugs used to reside.

No nets spun out to dry on racks
That stand like crosses on a grave,
And sounds of sparrows sift through cracks
Of an empty shed's weathered staves.

Smell of wood smoke in the distance,
Redolent of something I knew yesterday,
Takes me back there for an instant,
Where chubs were smoked and hung in gold display.

To see once more the tugs returning,
Splitting water from wooden hulls;
Hear once again the hungry calling,
Overhead, the white cloud of gulls.

Was there some parable in seagull song
Or in the banter of the men?
And din of diesels that chugged along,
Oil soaked, returning them home again.

Morning goes down like a sinking stone;
One old fish tug, all that remains,

Idle in her slip, moored alone,
Paint peeled, and forgotten by name.

A fish box, empty, gone to grey,
A sad reminder so it seems,
How everything must fade away
Like some old fisherman's dreams.

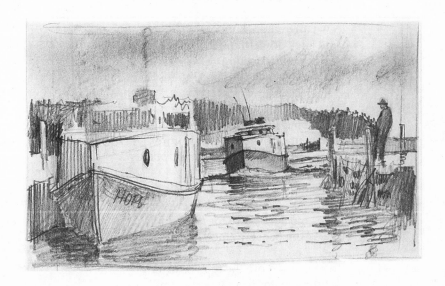

A Journey Through Time
(Porte des Morts Forest Preserve)
by Terrie Cooper

"One of the penalties of an ecological education is that one lives alone in a world of wounds. Much of the damage inflicted on land is quite invisible to the laymen."

—Aldo Leopold

I am forever grateful for the choice my mother made in 1970 that moved us from the suburbs of Chicago after her divorce to the nurturing cocoon of Door County, whose beauty and wildness provided great solace and a connection with something much greater than me. I have a deep-seated bond with this place that developed from a childhood spent immersed in the wilderness of northern Door, an intimacy that developed into a deep sense of longing that I felt throughout the 15 years I spent away from this place as an adult. I didn't know how much I needed Door, her wilderness, her waters, her rocky escarpments and miles of undeveloped shoreline. She grounded me and comforted me in a way no other place I lived ever could.

There is something sacred about this narrow fragile backbone of rock that is completely embraced by the glacial waters of Lake Michigan. For me, the true wilderness of Door County is found in the power and immensity of the inland freshwater sea that surrounds her shores and the splendid isolation that is created. The energy and everchanging moods of the lake, the ability to look out at a horizon devoid of any human objects, to see the moon rise over her eastern waters and the sun set over the her western waters, is to feel humbled and awed by the incomprehensible timeless forces that have created this place and the tenacity and resistance this fragile rocky peninsula and her necklace of islands have had against such powerful and constant agents of change.

Now, as I paddle along the rocky shores of the Porte des Morts Forest in the legendary waters of Death's Door, I think of the thousands who traveled before me, the Native Americans, French voyageurs, and early European settlers who laid their eyes upon the very same ancient white cedars I look at today clinging to the escarpment. The dark canopy of the trees along this shoreline, protected forever by a conservation easement with the Door County Land Trust, allow one a glimpse back in time when towering forests like these once completely covered the entire county. White pines, sugar maple, red oaks, beech, and hemlock 300–500 years old, home to the woodland caribou, moose, lynx, mountain lion, black bear, and timber wolves, spoke of the harmonious balance that existed for thousands of years between Door County's earliest human inhabitants and the land.

It is hard to believe that in less than 150 years we have cut over not only once, but in most places twice, the majestic forests that covered these lands. Between 1880–1910, in less than 30 years, the entire wooded interior of Door was clear cut by the lumber companies and settlers moving ever westward to supply a rapidly growing nation hungry for wood products. First the pines were cut and floated down the lakes to sawmills, then years later as docks were built and roads created, the hardwoods, which didn't float, were cut and loaded on steamers and transported south and westward. With the loss of their woodland habitat and increased hunting pressure from the throngs of new settlers, the woodland caribou, moose, timber wolf, mountain lion, and lynx were also lost from this landscape. In their place, the more adaptable white-tail deer, coyote, fox, porcupine, and raccoon flourished in the newly cut-over lands.

Lured by hopes of a more prosperous life, early pioneer families came to Door and spent thousands of hours of back-breaking labor pulling stumps to convert the treeless rocky soils into farmland, dairy pastures, and fruit orchards. It was soon discovered, however, that the glaciers had transported most of Door's topsoil south and eastward, and that the thin northern soils would never be ideal farmland. As quickly as these fields and orchards were abandoned, nature's pioneers, the juniper, sumac, aspen, white ash, white pine, and white cedars, reclaimed and converted these rocky soils back to what they are suited best for, growing forests.

In the past 30 years, a new type of settler has also been laying claim to these abandoned farmlands at an ever-increasing rate: thousands of people whose hearts (like my own) long for a bit of this paradise, a place of inspiration where nature's splendor dominates the landscape, a respite from the rigors of urban living.

With so much change already taking place on this narrow fragile peninsula in only the past 150 years, I find myself wondering how this place can retain its rural character, beauty, and ecological integrity when it lies only a four-hour drive north of the third most densely populated region in the United States. To get a perspective on the rate of change that is happening in the county, consider that in the 90 years between 1880–1970, 50 percent of our county's total housing units were built (10,000 of the 20,000 housing units that exist in Door County today). Between 1970–2000, in just 30 years 10,000 more housing units, another 50 percent of the county's total housing units, were built. This rate of development translates into an average of 111 new housing units per year being built during the county's first 90 years of housing growth (1880–1970), and 333 new housing units per year being built in the county in the last 30 years (1970–2000).

In addition, the number of tourists visiting the county has been growing at a similar rate. In 1980, the number of people visiting Door County was a half million; by 1990 this number rose to more than 1 million, and in 2005 this number has climbed to over 2.1 million (a 400 percent increase in only 25 years)!

And with this rapid influx of new visitors and residents come the trappings and burdens they were hoping to leave behind. More of Door's open spaces and wild places are becoming tamed, suburbanized, subdivided, and dominated by the presence of new homes, buildings, roads, lights, mowed lawns, tulips and daffodils. Domesticated and subdued, the wildness, the unencumbered vistas, the rural character, the very reasons we are drawn here, are being threatened by those who love her. We are loving her to death — Death's Door, the death of Door, a slow erosion of the qualities that make her so desirable.

What is it about human nature, that we are compelled to possess and change that which we love?

I know I too am guilty of this type of love. My desire and longing to return home to Door in 1999 meant another four-acre abandoned orchard now bears a new structure. The fields where the coyotes den, the rough-legged hawk and great horned owls hunt for meadow voles, and the monarchs feast on milkweed are now a little smaller thanks to me. I agonized over this decision, felt an enormous responsibility to give back more to this land than what I took, and am consequently assisting nature in restoring these old fields of European weeds and abandoned apple trees back to the white pine, hemlock, and hardwood forests that once covered these thin fragile soils.

I am humbled daily by the tenacity of nature to restore herself against what seem at times like the greatest odds. In my old fields under the newly established trees, remnants of woodland wildflowers, bloodroot, Solomon's seal, trillium and Canada mayflower, are reclaiming their rightful place. Viable seeds that have somehow been able to wait for years in the soils under the orchards that dominated this land for over 80 years have broken through the dense cover of European grasses and weeds: spotted knapweed, Queen Anne's lace, hawkweed, and clover, and found their way to the sunlight. Junipers cling to the shallow soils, slowly building up their fertility while providing a refuge from the voracious browsing of the white-tail deer, for the ash, white pine, and white cedar saplings on their way skyward.

Despite my fear that the tides of change sweeping over this place will greatly alter Door's landscapes as we know them today, it is in nature's tenacious ability to restore herself that I find hope and perspective, and recognize that humans' impact on this planet is but a blink of an eye when measured against the myriad geological and natural forces that have shaped this beautiful planet for millions of years.

At the very tip of the peninsula, where the turbulent waters of Green Bay collide with those of Lake Michigan in the strait known as Porte des Morts, several hundred acres of majestic unfragmented forest embrace the steep shoreline bluffs. Hemlock, beech, white pine, white cedar, and sugar maple that escaped the lumberman's saw are utilized by many species of birds as a stopover during migration and for critical nesting habitat. To date, the Door County Land Trust has protected 65 acres of Porte des Morts Forest from future development though conservation easements, and protection of another 30-acre tract is currently under way. Though the woodland caribou and lynx no longer roam these forests (a lone wolf, however, has been sighted here in the past few years), the Porte des Morts Forest offers one of the last best hopes for preserving a piece of Door County that has little changed since the days of Indians and French voyageurs.

I am in love with this place, I am in love with all these special wild places that define Door. They have shaped the person I am, the way I see the world, the passion I feel for my life's purpose, the sadness I feel at times in how quickly things are changing here and the joy I feel in the critically important work I do.

My Country, Which Is of Trees
by Frances May

Everything on this great green earth is alive —
alive in a planetary way, holding our truth.
You hear how the leaves come awake in the night
like people we know and marvel at their industry,
but trees in the summer can be deeply disturbed
and keep us under anxiety all through the night
in our minds that they cannot reach in our sounds
but rattle, thrash and groan among their ancestry
locked in boards of houses and barns, our churches
until the young shingles fly away in the night.
In the morning elms may be darkened and silent
and the glorious maples are bedraggled creatures
combing their leaves in a seemingly penitent air.
In their shadow-height and their lack-luster gratitude
the trees still shed their beneficence for all comers.

And the winter seems to be the long night for trees,
cold, wet snow creeping around their earth bound feet,
ice water dripping down bare limbs to a sodden ground
while they wait, wordless, for the sun, moods of its own.
Our alien chatter, if it could pierce the bark of a tree
has no foreseeable effect on these natives we use for shade
and comfort according to the old rabbinical bards of nature
but the elements imposed into the bodies and blood of trees
are here for lifetimes, like our birds, jewels of the air.

Porte des Morts Park
by Barbara Larsen

It looks like an abandoned battlefield.
Thundering waves once swept in
to bite their teeth into overhanging ledges
where old warrior cedars defended life.
Their horny claws cling to crevices in rocks.
Their roots crawl over one another
like nesting vipers.

Upon the rocky highland
the wind army still deploys its forces
in a battle that never ceases.
Old tree soldiers bend to its will
but do not capitulate.
Bowed low to the earth
they keep on resisting,
keep fighting for life.

November, Porte des Morts
Judith Roy

Under the inland sea
sailors lie, pure, skeletal
as the proud and crucified trees
beyond the stony beach.

Along this coast
wind sounds an autumnal dirge,
counterpoint to the cadence of waves.
Exhausted leaves return to earth.

There is a cleansing in this time and place
where a lone gull still calls
and rain falls welcome on the land.

The Waters of Door County
by Jim Griffith

The waters of Lake Michigan and Green Bay encompass Door County. Nowhere in the county are we far from these waters. The exhilarating, yet foreboding view of the bluffs on the Bay side of the peninsula are virtually unchanged from that seen by the Potawatomi Indians two hundred years ago. Without its extensive shoreline, Door would be no more memorable a county than Dodge or Richland. Lake Michigan and its Green Bay appendage provide the county's cooling breezes, its recreation, its character. Much of my time "in" Door County has been spent in the waters around it, inevitably in a sailboat.

One occasion, forever etched on my memory was in mid-September, 1999. My sons Sam, Jack, and I, sailors with a combined 150 years experience between us, chartered the Merlin, a 32-foot sloop. We share a desire, not uncommon to sailors, to be away from the land with its bustle, is disorder, its responsibilities. Leaving from Sister Bay with perfect weather, the Eagle and Ellison Bluffs were soon clearly defined astern, their indented silhouettes resembling two streamlined locomotives. With a moderate beam wind, we knifed through friendly waters and reached Jackson Harbor on Washington Island in time for a swim. Having a certain restaurant in mind for dinner, I called the Island's sole cab company for a 7:00 pickup. The dispatcher informed me that the cab company closed at 6:00 — winter hours, already - but that if we could be ready by 6:30 her husband would pick us up. It was then 6:10, but I assured her we could be ready. Her husband arrived punctually and told us, "I'll take you there, but I think they're closed for the season." He did and they were. As an alternative, our driver — by this time our benefactor and friend as well — suggested a restaurant that he had formerly owned. We readily agreed and on arrival asked him to join us for a drink. He did so. The beer was good. The large pizza that we consumed at the bar was even better. At the end of the evening, the restaurant owner-waiter at his suggestion drove us back to the Merlin. It is personal touches such as these that endear Door County to the city dweller, whether from Chicago or from Wausau.

The following day we headed for Fayette, Michigan, 28 miles to the northeast in a moderate breeze. Besides the interesting sailing waters, Fayette offered a chance to view a mining village deserted in the first decade of the 19th century. We had no sooner moored at this desolate spot than the wind changed from a tranquil ten to an ominous 35 mile northerly. We had our traditional drink, ate aboard, then slept an apprehensive sleep.

When we awoke, the wind was unabated. Leaving our mooring in a tight natural harbor, we found that the linkage between the rudder and the ship's wheel had ceased to function. We quickly jammed in a tiller so that we could control the boat manually.

With seven-foot seas behind us, our towed dingy behaved ominously, rushing at the Merlin on the crest of each following wave. We considered returning to the deserted Fayette harbor, but decided against it. The dingy slowly filled with water, then submerged. I expected the added weight to pull the stem(holding the eye and thus the tender rope) out of the dingy. It did not happen. We started our engine, turned 180 degrees into the wind, and after a ten-minute fight in the seven-foot seas, we succeeded in restoring the dingy's buoyancy.

We sailed on. Each wave threw us toward some protrusion in the cockpit. For hours, our legs and bodies were constantly braced. Slowly, numbness set in.

On reaching the Wisconsin peninsula, we had gone more than thirty grueling up and down miles, but were far from Sister Bay. Much closer was the Cedar Grove harbor, very small and only partially protected, but I had been there before. Sam and I opted for the nearer harbor. Jack told us we were out of our minds, that the farther harbor was safer. Having no real captain, the majority ruled. We doused our sails and started the motor. Somehow, I was elected to make the mooring in spite of Sam's proficiency with his own boat of similar size, but of far different below-the-waterline silhouette. The harbor mouth was narrower than the length of our boat. I steered for its windward side, but the wind shoved our bow into the cement piling. Sam, at the split controls, reversed the engine in a fraction of a second and we escaped major damage. My second effort brought us to safety. Weary hands secured the Marlin to the sea wall. No surges of the sea could inhibit the sleep of three dead tired sailors that night.

Sailing between the peninsula and Washington Island we had gone through Porte des Morts of excellent fishing when the waters are calm, but the graveyard of many large sailing ships as well as some under motor, "Death's Door." The month of November has taken a particularly heavy toll.

Two more tranquil bodies of water are Eagle Harbor off Ephraim and Europe Lake, bounded on its eastern shore by Newport State Park. Eagle Harbor is home port for the Flying Scott fleet of 19-foot racing sailboats. Only infrequently do the winds penetrate the high bluffs that make Eagle Harbor a normally placid pond. Many times in Ephraim my wife and I have chartered a small boat to sail to Horseshoe Island and explore the ruins of several old buildings hidden among the dense cedars. A more venturesome race is the Hook Race that sails roughly 200 miles from Racine through the Porte des Morts passage, around Chambers Island, and down to Sturgeon Bay.

Europe Lake is the northernmost of twelve interior lakes in the County. It has obvious advantages for the beginner who may not need a life jacket since, in the event of capsize, to save one's life he has only to stand up and wade ashore. The neck of land on its eastern shore contains fine hiking trails, some of which lead in just a couple hundred yards to the extensive unsullied shore of Lake Michigan — unsullied, that is, except by an occasional mass of rotting algae.

While both the Michigan and the Bay sides of the peninsula have their perils for boaters, it is the Bay side that abounds with harbors. It is there, too, that the waters are warmer and the topography more rugged and more attractive to tourists. While the Michigan side has many bays, their waters are shoal with the exception of the well developed Baileys Harbor.

As the Door becomes more intensively developed, the threats to its adjacent waters increase commensurately. We have seen a dismaying increase in beach closings and advisories. In the five years ending in 2003, Wisconsin as a whole experienced a seven-fold increase in beach closings and advisories. Door County alone inched up slightly from 78 to 80 in '05 over the preceding year. These closings and advisories are but the tip of the iceberg. E.coli levels vary greatly from day to day, yet most Wisconsin counties test only weekly. In Door and Sheboygan Counties, no testing is done under county auspices, but the Department of Natural Resources monitors at Nicolet Bay Beach in the Peninsula State Park, while the City of Sheboygan monitors at its two beaches. Thus, the closing-advisory figures for Door are useful, not as an accurate gage of the beaches that should have been closed, but of the existence of a festering problem.

Another source of beach and water contamination is agricultural runoff from Wisconsin's four counties bordering the Bay as well as from Michigan's Menominee County. Its source: pig and cattle manure. This is exacerbated by the absence of contour plowing on the hillsides and the lack of effective state and federal regulation.

Affecting the near shore waters and, to a lesser extent, the beaches, is mercury pollution, chiefly airborne from coal-fired factories. While there is currently no mercury advisory for Green Bay, there are advisories for other Wisconsin lakes and for our upstream Great Lake, Superior.

One bright spot: our waters so far have not been subjected to drilling for oil, this destructive extraction having been outlawed by Wisconsin, Michigan, and Illinois. Indiana, despite its limited shore line, remains a potential threat. The zebra mussel through its larva continues to spread from Lake Michigan to the smaller Wisconsin lakes, including those of the Door, as boats with infested bottoms are removed from Lake Michigan and launched on hitherto uninfested bodies of water. Lower lake levels have been documented over the long term, albeit with shorter term ups and downs. These lower levels result in shoreline and seawall exposure. An accord has now been signed by the governors of all states bordering on the Great Lakes which offers some, but far from complete, protection against the ever-increasing demands for lake water by residential and commercial users.

Like the canary in the coal mine, marine fauna are the early warning system for the County's waters. We have seen fish with cancers and cormorant chicks with crossed bills in Green Bay. Nor is the eastern shore exempt from signs of water degradation. Vast masses of rotting and smelly algae collect on the shore in Newport State Park. In other areas, salt and oil might be absorbed before they run off to contaminate streams and bays. Not so in the Door where a few inches of topsoil are underlaid by largely impervious dolomite bedrock. These substances, together with any intact e.coli flow directly into the Door's waters. When the ground is frozen, this runoff is exacerbated.

While PCB contamination from the Fox River has abated, the root causes of beach closings remain partly unknown and largely unchecked. A remedy has been slow in coming. Subsequent to a doubling of Wisconsin beach closings in 2000, the state DNR applied to the USEPA for a grant under the Beach Environmental Assessment & Coastal Health Act. Four years later that application is still pending.

There are some remedial steps where the Door County resident can make a difference. We can be sure our septic systems are not overloaded and in good repair. We can switch from salt to sand on our roads. Hybrid or fuel efficient cars and four-cycle outboards can reduce toxic emissions. When considering a leaf blower, go electric. The organic garden and lawn will reduce herbicide runoff. Our County Board members should be encouraged to allocate funds for multiple beach testing sites on a daily basis during the swimming season. Strict enforcement of building and zoning codes are essential to check overdevelopment.

Development pressure will continue, however, until our nation obtains better control of its burgeoning population, both by guarding its borders and by more pervasive birth control. The earth, after all, is a finite place. At some time our residents need merely to say "enough." Without this will, thirty years will see the Bay side become a solid phalanx of condos and fifty will see high rises similar to Chicago's north side along the lake. The Bay will be invisible to the motorist on Route 42.

When we think of Door County our thoughts may well turn to fish. We may buy fresh fish direct from the fishermen at Gill's Rock and smoked fish all along our two major highways. The fish boils at the White Gull Inn in Ephraim or the Viking in Ellison Bay are a must for the tourist. Sport fishermen converge from four states to supplement their larders and to lend plausibility to their tales of the big one that got away.

The marine environment of the Door is fulfilling and beautiful, but nevertheless a fragile one. Its health is dependent on the constant attention and effort of each of us.

Island Wild

by Julian Hagen

"Northern Lights" was written in 1973 in the barn while milking cows before going to school. I was a junior in high school. I smile thinking back because a milking machine works in 2/4 time and the song is written in 3/4 time. Music was so important on the Island both for entertainment as well as a way to interact.

Many Island nights were spent sitting around a campfire or in a living room playing and singing. It was a magical time. I just decided one day to try and write a song and did. "Northern Lights" was my 2nd composition.

Ah, the words. I was wise beyond my years. My youthful outlook was not cluttered with all of the "stuff" that gets in the way as we age. I'm not sure about the idea behind the song — Living it up while we can, celebrating friends, life and nature. I just remember being aware of how blessed I was. In the first verse, I refer to the northern lights. I remember getting my sister out of bed at 1 in the morning to go for a motorcycle ride while the lights were dancing in the sky. I had a 1964 Honda Dream with a single carb, and we would ride along with the headlights off.

A number of my songs are inspired by island life and experiences. Sadly my "wild" is different than the "wild" of the Island and the county of today. Back then, we lived predominately off and with the land, were intricately linked to our neighbors. We could walk across the Island and not be considered "trespassers." My idea of "wild" also involves a way of life. Changes on the island happened quite subtly. It was like being next to someone growing older. You may not notice the changes, but for those who are more aware or come back after an extended period of time, the change can't be missed. We certainly can't go back. The same for the Island. Once damaged or gone, whether open places to roam, species, silence, dark skies, fresh air, or fresh water, it is so hard to repair and perhaps impossible to regain.

Northern Lights
by Julian Hagen

Laughing and dancing, yet tears in my eyes,
I've watched the Northern Lights dance in the skies
To a simple freedom song

Twisting and turning, yet calm all around,
They've made my feet never touch the ground.
Yes, they've made me dance along.

Chorus
Because we'll never have this time to live again,
So why not live it up while we can
'Fore there's less time than before
And I don't know how much more
And I know we'll never have this time again.

Fresh smell of wood smoke invading my mind
Makes me remember all the good times
That I've spent here with my friends.

Talking and dreaming of what we could be
If we could just find life's simple key
To make it never end.

Chorus

Saving the Forest
by Alice D'Alessio

On my desk, a hawk's skull
thin as parchment
rests in its pottery cradle beside
the ivory clenched talons;
acorns and fluted walnuts
sleep in an oak-leaf nest
their tasks undone.

Gleanings from the forest,
they whisper of soft rain, wild wind,
their fiber woven from millennia of adaptations—
spring's wanton surge and autumn ripening.
I keep them close at hand.

If I store them
in stoppered urns
hand-painted with Druid symbols

If I take them out when the moon
silvers the birch,
rub my fingers on their sacred skin,
turn slowly around three times
chanting the dove's slow plaint,

will the stealthy ones cease their invasion?
Will the earth cool, the rains come?

Will this be enough?

Afterword: The Lake Effect
by Norbert Blei

Whether you've lived here your entire life, summered here for fifty years, or are coming into the county for the first time, the moment you see water that surrounds the peninsula, that hugs its harbors and small towns, its islands, its jagged shores of sand, pebbles, and bluffs, that's the moment you fall in love with this place for the first time or all over again.

While much of this book voices a concern over land preservation in Door County, without the backdrop and presence of water, be it swamp, creek, river, inland lake or the great blue waters of Lake Michigan, the land has little distinction from peace-in-the-rural anywhere USA, which needs our appreciation and attention as well. But is nowhere close to the unique nature of the landscape here, the give and take of land and water, the seasons, light and darkness, past and present, how it all comes together and speaks to the spirit of place within us.

The soul of this peninsula is water from beginning to end.

Our whole history is water.

From the time of Indian tribes to French explorers, from fishermen to sailors, from sailing vessels to lighthouse keepers, from shipwrecked schooners to early tourists aboard passenger steamers, from pioneer days to the present, you can't read a history, a memoir, a poem, or an early post card that fails to pay homage and attention to the wonder of water on these craggy shores.

In H. R. Holand's final chapter "Toilers of the Sea" of his history of Door County, *Old Peninsula Days* (1925), he concludes that as much history here was enacted upon water as land, fishermen, lighthouse keepers, sailors and sea captains with cargos of timber, sea squalls and gales and the dangerous passage through Death's Door. It was always about water:

It is also preeminently the home of the sailor. Door County boys are nearly all the sons of fishermen or of sailors turned farmers, and with their constant childhood vision of the sea they turn as naturally to a seafaring life

*as the Welsh turn to mining. On all sorts of crafts they are to be found, from
the huge carferries of the Great Lakes crashing their course through three feet
of ice with thirty loaded freight cars in the hold, to the mammoth ocean liners
that ply between foreign ports. But whether in Santiago or Singapore the
Door County sailor looks back to his home with its headlands and variously
indented shores, its forests and green fields, and its glorious sunsets, as the
fairest spot on earth.*

So just what is it we are committed to put into trust, to preserve:
land or water? Or are they one and the same, given the geology and
geography of this county?

How sacred is water? How precious will it become in a world running out of resources, a world running out of everything but hate and
greed?

Peninsula: Latin: *paene*, almost + *insula*, island

"Almost Island." That's us. How we know it. How it appears and
welcomes us by water and land.

I remember coming into the county for the first time in the 1950s.
It was sunny. It was hot. It was a long drive from Chicago then. No
interstate. It was probably late July or August. "Going to Wisconsin."
Not just Lake Geneva, where everyone seemed headed every summer,
or any of the small lakes over and across the Illinois/Wisconsin border.
No, not *that* Wisconsin. But further. "Way up there"—as we saw it
then. Like the north woods.

The appeal, as I recall: cherry orchards and cherry pie; fresh air
and the smell of pine; summer air 'conditioned' by the cool waters of
Lake Michigan; eating fresh fish and homemade pies at authentic,
local restaurants like the Brookside Tea Garden and the Knudson
House, where you ate at long tables, family style, with strangers. At
night, you slept in a screened-in back porch of a cottage on the shore in
Ephraim and listened to the sound of the waves lulling you to sleep.

While the old, beautiful lattice-steel, Michigan St. Bridge of Sturgeon Bay remains a controversial issue in the county these days (Fix
it!/Tear the damn thing down!) in those days, it was the only passage
to the peninsula by car, and as magnificent an entrance as anyone
could imagine. A throw-back in time. A Door County icon, to my mind,
which should be treasured. It was what we watched for, the sight of
that silver bridge, to confirm the fact we were here. We had indeed
arrived.

And then the sound of wheels going over the grates, crossing the
Sturgeon Bay Ship Canal, where Green Bay and Lake Michigan meet
and the beauty of water beneath us, beside us, ahead, sparkling and
alive, breaking in the wake of speedboats, fishtugs, and the serene
glide of sailboats, making their way to deeper waters in the wind. If

you were lucky, you arrived at the bridge precisely at the moment the bridge tender had to raise it, give it a set of iron wings, allowing a large sailing vessel or ship to pass through.

That was the baptism. The ritual of water. And the further up the county you drove, other manifestations awaited you along shorelines, harbors, to the very tip of the peninsula, where Porte des Morts awaited you, and beyond that a journey by ferry to Washington Island. Water, water, and the redemption of more water.

I could map out the entire county, illustrating by word my favorite views. The places I need to go, to see and feel again, for whatever reasons. The sculptural powers of water at Cave Point, the force of wind and water off Lake Michigan on the peninsula's eastern shore...border's on a religious experience, if you're there at the right time. But better to seek and find your own wild and holy places here, blessed by water.

The first of the two great views every traveler comes across, carries with him forever, is certainly the sight of Ephraim coming down the hill, down Highway 42, around the shoreline, along the beach, coming into the 'Little White Village' itself...church steeples, Wilson's, the village hall...radiating such history and beauty. The water's mark... Eagle Harbor, Eagle Bluff, Horseshoe Island...all the way to old Anderson Dock. Breathtaking...day and night. Spring, summer, winter, fall. The one village on the entire peninsula that will never let you go.

The Sister Bay shoreline has grown increasingly more open, more beautiful through the years. We are glad to have the view we have of sunsets and water as we drive by or leave the car and linger there along the shore awhile, but it will never be Ephraim.

Second to none is the view from the top of the hill in Ellison Bay which begs newcomers to slow, stop, take a photograph, and natives to pause and give thanks—this is their own backyard to enjoy every day of their lives. This is Ellison Bay/Green Bay, seen from on high— bird's eye, God's eye view. And what you see is...what the Indian, first settler must have seen and felt as he stood upon the same spot, looked out over the great good earth, the splendor of water and sky for as far as the eye could see.

There are some things in the natural world you simply cannot take home in a photograph, recreate in any way close to the moment of awareness. Things better left alone. Water is one of them. We know what it continues to tell us. The same old story...ours since the beginning of time.

It beckons.

And keeps calling us home.

Contributors' Notes

SHARON AUBERLE lives in Sister's Bay and the drought-stricken Southwest and is deeply drawn to the renewal of spirit that the seasons of Lake Michigan provide. "It would be difficult to choose a favorite. The glittering shards of ice in winter; explosions of wildflowers in spring, the magnificent migrating waterfowl of autumn — all inspire my poetry, while the clear green waters restore my parched soul." Her poetry appears in three recent anthologies: *Woman Prayer, Literary Lunch* (Knoxville Writer's Guild) and *Common Ground Anthology*, and various publications, including *American Poetry Review*.

NORBERT BLEI lives in Ellison Bay. www.bleidoorcountytimes.com ; www.norbertblei.com

LORAINE BRINK grew up on a farm and has a great love for the environment and all of its creatures. "Reading about the possible extinction of the Hines Emerald Dragonfly caused me to muse about different attitudes toward extinction," she says.

DAN BURKE has served as executive director of the Door County Land Trust since 1996 and previously served on the land trust's board of directors for two years. Under his leadership, the land trust has evolved from an all-volunteer organization with 250 acres protected to an organization that has preserved more than 3,800 acres throughout the county and that has the support of more than 1,500 members. In 2004, the Door County Land Trust was named Wisconsin's Land Trust of the Year. Dan and his wife, Heidi, live in downtown Sturgeon Bay where they raise their two children, MacKenzie and Nathan.

TERRIE COOPER grew up in Ellison Bay. She left for college in 1979 and worked as a naturalist and environmental educator throughout Wisconsin for more than 15 years. She has a master's degree in natural resources and environmental education from the University of Wisconsin-Stevens Point and a bachelor of science in conservation, biology and secondary education from the University of Wisconsin—Madison. In 1998, Terrie co-founded a land trust in Sheboygan, which began a new career for her in the land trust field. In 1999, Terrie returned home to Door County to work for the Door County Land Trust and spends her free time kayaking, hiking and exploring this beautiful place.

ALICE D'ALESSIO is a former corporate communications director and publications editor. She divides her time between writing poetry and managing the family land near Ridgeway, Wisconsin. She is actively involved in conservation and restoration projects on the property, a future land trust site. Her biography, *Uncommon Sense: The Life of Marshall Erdman,* was published by Trails Press in September, 2003; her chapbook, *A Blessing of Trees* was published by Cross+Roads Press in April 2004 and was the winner of the Council for Wisconsin Writers Posner Book-length Poetry Award. She has published in various small journals and has won a Muse Prize from the Wisconsin Fellowship of Poets and various other statewide awards.

JUDE GENEREAUX has published in *The Poetry of Cold, The Wisconsin Poets' Calendar, Hummingbird* and other publications. "For a short time, I had the pleasure of living in Baileys Harbor, an area surrounded by water. Besides its well known harbor and beaches, Baileys has an abundance of swampy acres, thick with cedars, brackish motes, and frogs and peepers. Spring evenings were filled with such an abundance of sound, one is drawn outdoors to stand, listen and count the blessings of darkness. And write about it."

JIM GRIFFITH has sailed in Door County waters for four decades. He is a retired Chicago lawyer. As a founder of the Committee on Lake Michigan Pollution, he organized three televised picketings of U.S. Steel that led to its cleanup of its South Works plant. He was president of the Lake Michigan Federation (now the Alliance for the Great Lakes) in 1973 and again from 1992–1994.

JULIAN HAGEN is a fifth generation Washington Islander who lives on the family homestead where his great grandfather settled in 1880. He loves the Island and continues to write and perform. More can be learned at www.julianhagen.com.

TRYGVIE JENSEN was born and raised on Washington Island. He has a strong love and appreciation towards his family, Norwegian heritage, and nature. His book, *Wooden Boats and Iron Men: History of Commercial Fishing in Northern Door County and Washington Island,* is scheduled to be published this year.

JENS HANSEN is a musician/songwriter and a native of Washington Island. He has a deep appreciation for the wetlands of this country and an even deeper concern for our most precious resource, our fresh water.

LAUREL HAUSER is the membership coordinator of the Door County Land Trust. She has lived in Door County since 1986 and resides in Sturgeon Bay with her husband and two children.

CHARLOTTE E. JOHNSTON: "Door County is my home away from home, a tranquil place where nature and one's notice of it abounds. At Bjorkebower, a nature journal lies open and a camera awaits to record the latest observance. A nature writing experience at The Clearing (in Ellison Bay) opened my eyes to the delicate balance of life in a boreal forest near Lake Michigan, a few miles east of Sister Bay. On the day of our hike, I felt uprooted from my usual surroundings, much like the storm-toppled cedars of my poem."

BARBARA LARSEN lives on a wooded bluff overlooking the water of Green Bay. She attributes the inspiration for her writing to this place of ever-changing sky and waterscapes. Many of her nature poems about the beauty and unique environment of Door County are included in her latest book, *All In Good Season.*

ESTELLE LAUTER has been a part-time resident of Door County since 1971 and now lives year-round on the land that she and her husband have placed in the land trust to protect Ephraim swamp. She first saw the pictographs that appear in this poem on a walk with Terrie Cooper in May 2003 and wrote the poem for her son's wedding that September. She was drawn to the images for all the reasons that appear in the poem but also because she has studied Native cultures of the Great Lakes and finds in them a source of courage and hope.

ROY LUKES, a Door County resident since 1968, has been an advocate for nature and conservation for 50 years. He was the resident naturalist and manager of the Ridges Sanctuary for 27 years. His weekly "Nature-Wise" column in the *Door County Advocate* has sought to teach about our natural world and encourage good stewardship of the land and all of its resources. He has written five books, teaches outdoor education classes, leads field trips for the Door County Festival of Nature and presents illustrated lectures on many aspects of nature.

FRANCES MAY of Sturgeon Bay is the prize-winning author of six books of poetry. Her recent book, *The Rain Barrel,* was published by Cross+Roads Press. Frances died in 2004.

RALPH MURRE is an architect and mariner, a father and grandfather, a poet and dreamer who lives near Jacksonport, Wisconsin. His moods often mirror those of Lake Michigan. Some of his writings appear in *Backstreet Quarterly, Clark Street Review, Cliffs Surroundings, Free Verse, Poetry Motel and Wisconsin Poets' Calendar.* He tramps the woods and shore and shares his findings with some reluctance, fearing the loss of places of solitude.

JIM OLSEN is a native of Sturgeon Bay, built ships for a time there, and then moved on to buildings.

BILL OLSON is the former head of the Washington Island Writers Group and has lived on Washington Island since 1989. He has published several poetry, fiction and non-fiction books and serves as a volunteer for many island organizations.

SUE PETERSON has lived across the street from the Anderson pond property, now known as the Ephraim Preserve at Anderson Pond since 1973. She has walked, skied, ice skated, picnicked on the property and especially watched birds over the years. These essays are expanded versions of notes written in her bird journals. She was active, with many others, in helping the Door County Land Trust acquire the Anderson pond property for permanent protection. She is the author of the book of poems, *Preparing the Fields.*

GEORGE K. PINNEY, head of the Door County Parks Department since 1995, was born and raised in the county, both parents dating back to the mid-1800s. His mother's family were orchard growers and father's family started the Evergreen Nursery in 1864.

RICHARD PURINTON is married to Mary Jo (Richter), is the father of three children and has lived on Main Road, Washington Island, for 30 years. He graduated from UW-Madison School of Journalism and is a U.S. Navy veteran and is president and licensed captain for the Washington Island Ferry Line.

MARK RADDATZ: "I've been fishing the Green Bay/Lake Michigan waters since childhood and the streams (Hibbard, Heinz, Rieboldt and the Mink) since I was a young adult. My love of fishing and the outdoors was passed on to me by my father and grandfather, and I've been teaching it to my children and hopefully someday to my grandchildren. I am a chef and a singer-songwriter by trade."

NANCY RAFAL has lived in Door County for a dozen years. She has always sought the natural world and endeavors to be a better steward for the land each day. She has been a Door County Land Trust board member and volunteers on various Land Trust projects. "I am fortunate to live in an area with much protected land and I want to inform others of the need to protect even more land."

JUDY ROY is a poet who lives in the boreal forest north of Baileys Harbor. A co-author of the chapbook, *Slightly Off Q*, she has read her work throughout Wisconsin and has been published in poetry journals within and beyond the state.

GLORIA SMALL and her husband, Lou, moved to Washington Island from Illinois in 1980 with their children. Gloria recently retired from teaching elementary school, the last twenty years at the island school. She is a frequent contributor to the *Washington Island Observer*, the island newspaper, and a volunteer for many island organizations.

KAREN YANCEY is a former writer for the *Milwaukee Journal/Sentinel* and *Chicago Tribune*. She has a master's degree from Northwestern University's Medill School of Journalism. She has developed and lead environmental education programs for elementary and high school students for more than a decade. She and her family spend their summers on Washington Island in their 100-year-old renovated farmhouse. She is on the board of directors of the Door County Land Trust and heads its Washington Island Project, which has helped protect more than 500 acres on the island since 2000.

Proceeds from this book will benefit the Door County Land Trust's
20th Anniversary Capital Campaign.